How
to Be a
Dog

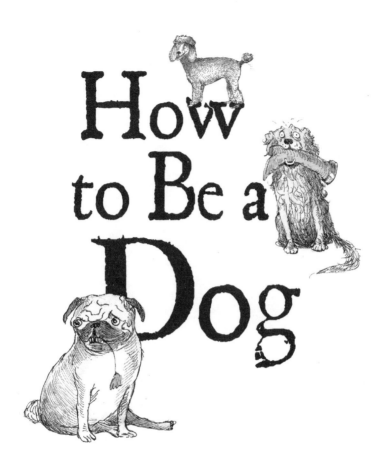

How to Be a Dog

Maxwell Woofington's Guide to Living with Humans and Getting the Upper Paw

As told to Mark Leigh

Michael O'Mara Books Limited

First published in Great Britain in 2015 by
Michael O'Mara Books Limited
9 Lion Yard
Tremadoc Road
London SW4 7NQ

A CIP catalogue record for this book is available from the British Library.

Papers used by Michael O'Mara Books Limited are natural,
recyclable products made from wood grown in sustainable
forests. The manufacturing processes conform to the
environmental regulations of the country of origin.

ISBN: 978-1-78243-417-7 in hardback print format
ISBN: 978-1-78243-419-1 in e-book format

1 3 5 7 9 10 8 6 4 2

Designed and typeset by Ana Bjezancevic

All photos from Shutterstock, apart from those of the author, © Mark Leigh

Illustrations by Gillian Johnson

Printed and bound by CPI Group (UK) Ltd, Croydon, CR0 4YY

www.mombooks.com

INTRODUCTION

You're a dog. We all know it's demeaning to have to eat from a bowl on the floor and pee in the street in public. Get over it. Once you deal with these realities of life, the most important thing to learn is not just how to co-exist with humans, it's how to ensure you become the alpha male or female of the pack. And by pack, I mean the family you live with. And that's where this book comes in.

Much more than simply a comprehensive A-to-Z guide to life as man's best friend, *How to Be a Dog* also gives advice on how to put up with humans and manipulate them into doing exactly what you want. The secret? All it takes is a combination of dogged determination, canine cunning and good old-fashioned guilt, using your puppy-dog eyes as often as possible to get humans completely under your thumb (well, if you had thumbs, that is).

These invaluable insights are drawn from my own experiences and also from consulting with my many four-legged pals. You can read their views and observations in the series of Canine Comments that appear throughout the book.

If you're worried about making the transformation from a pet who is at its owner's beck and call to one that reaches the dizzy heights of Top Dog, let me leave you with just one thought: if you were out and saw two creatures and one of them pooped, and the other then carried the poop, who would you think was in charge?

Maxwell Woofington
Surrey, England

AGE: DOG vs HUMAN

By the time this book is published, I'll be seven and a half, which in human years is forty-five years old. That means I'm the exact doggy equivalent of Matthew McConaughey, Matt Damon and Gerard Butler. Helloooooooo, ladies!

Now, at this point you're probably saying, 'Hold on a mo, 7½ x 7 = 52½. That Maxwell Woofington is always lying about his age!' But I'm not.

The idea that you simply multiply your dog age by seven to convert it into human years is wrong. There's no universal formula … It all depends on your breed, weight and life expectancy. For example, a dachshund exactly the same age as me would be about forty-two in human years, while an Irish wolfhound would be sixty-four. And sorry, Great Danes: if you're the same age as me, then in human years you're, well … let's just say you'd better get your affairs in order.

CANINE COMMENT

Millie I'm only two in dog years, but because of my breed everyone calls me old. It's not fair.

ALPHA MALES/FEMALES

There's only room for one dominant male or female in your household – and that needs to be you.

That's why it's vital, as soon as you can in your relationship with your human family, to show your owners just who's boss. By this I don't mean angrily growling every time they give you a command or nipping their fingers when they try and take away your favourite chew toy. That won't necessarily show them who's boss. In fact, it could very well show them who's going to be taken to the animal shelter.

Remember, dominance doesn't have to mean aggression. One of the best ways to assert your position as alpha male or female is by making sure you **get your own way.**

Try this simple test to see if you're really Top Dog.

Are you the alpha male or alpha female of the family?

How many commands do you obey?
- A. Most of them
- B. Half of them
- C. Meh …

What do you call the main human in your household?
- A. Master or Mistress
- B. Owner
- C. That schmuck

Where do you sleep each night?

    A. On the landing

    B. On my owner's bed

    C. In my owner's bed

How do you signal to your owner that you want to go outside?

    A. I don't. I go out when he allows me to

    B. Run around in circles and bark

    C. I just give them 'that' look

When are you taken for walkies?

    A. When my owner decides it's time

    B. Twice a day

    C. Thirty seconds after I stare at my leash and start barking my head off

Where do you travel in the car?

    A. In the boot, behind a dog guard

    B. On the back seat, secured by a safety belt

    C. Car? Good luck getting me in one of those!

How do you respond when your owner asks, 'Who's a good boy?'

    A. 'I am! I am! I am! I am! I am!'

    B. 'It's me. I'm the good boy!'

    C. 'You talkin' to me? You talkin' to ME?'

How do you react when your owners go out?

    A. I lie by the front door and whine

B. I sleep or play with my toys. Every now and then I might look out of the window

C. They've gone out? I hadn't noticed

RESULTS

Mainly As

You're more of a pussy than a dog. Grow some! (A human figure of speech, and especially ironic if you've just been neutered.)

Mainly Bs

While not alpha status at the moment, adopting a surlier attitude, stealing food off plates and exhibiting ambivalence towards the concept of 'fetch' will help you grow into this role.

Mainly Cs

With that combination of self-assurance and arrogance, when it comes to exerting your authority on the household, you're definitely Best in Show.

CANINE COMMENT

Zeus Of course I'm the alpha male. What does it look like?

See also *Packs, maintaining your position in*

ANAL GLANDS

To be frank (and it's difficult not to be when discussing our anuses), anal glands are a complete pain in the arse. To make them sound less unpleasant, your owner might refer to them as 'scent glands', but however you wrap them up, they're the same thing: two small paired sacs either side of the anus that empty out a liquid containing pheromones, which allow us to mark our territory.

Usually the anal glands empty automatically when we poop and we don't need to give them a second thought. Sometimes, though, like if our poop is runny, there's not enough pressure and they don't drain. You'll know when that happens because of a feeling of irritation and discomfort. Your owner will know it because he'll see you've stopped wagging your tail, you're dragging your bottom along the floor and you're trying to bite or scratch it – or because there's a really disgusting pungent fishy smell coming from your butt.

Whatever the sign (and let's hope for everyone involved it's not the last one), this is an aspect of our lives where we definitely need human help. Don't worry, it's a simple enough process to drain the sacs.

If you're fortunate, your owner will take you to the vet (one of the rare occasions I'll say that). If you're less fortunate, your owner will attempt the procedure himself. While this will help you bond, it is important to remember that inserting a lubricated gloved finger into your anus and poking it around is best left to someone who attended veterinary college. It is not a task for someone whose first thought is, 'I'll give it a go.'

BALL THROWERS

You'll recognize these devices by two things. The first is their appearance: brightly coloured pieces of plastic with a long handle and a scoop at the end. The second is their effect: making you run farther than you would like in order to retrieve a tennis ball.

Female owners like them because it helps them throw the ball a good enough distance for their dog to chase; male owners like them because it hides the fact that they, as they'd say, 'throw like a girl'.

See also *Fetch*

BANDANAS AND KERCHIEFS

Like collars, costumes and coats, these accessories are yet another example of the annoying human affectation of dressing us up to project their own personalities on to us. In this case, they want us to look like the James Dean of Dalmatians or the Marlon Brando of beagles – furless human cultural icons. If you're the rebellious type then that's fine. Even if you're not, you can probably get away with this look if you belong to travellers or if your owner is someone who goes across the country by boxcar (which, it must be said, is not a particularly common mode of transport these days). For the rest of us, it's important to be your own dog and wriggle out of this fashion faux pas as soon as possible. All it will do is make you look like you've got a serviette tucked into your collar. Not so much badass gang member as messy eater.

CANINE COMMENT

Woody The saying 'rebel without a paws' ceases to be funny the second time you hear it …

BARKING

As barking is the main way we communicate with humans, it's important that owners know the subtleties of the doggy language so that they will be able to correctly understand not just the difference between a yip and a yap or a whine and a howl, but also pick up on the changes in pitch and tempo, too. It is a big ask for humans to get to grips with such intricacies, but being consistent in how we bark is the quickest way they will learn, which in turn is the best way to get them to understand what we want (or don't want).

Knowing how the doggy language is construed by humans can be complicated, and there's a lot to remember, so I've written this handy guide to communication between the species.

Know your yip from your yap:
My handy guide to dog talk

Sound	When you might use it	What it means in human terms
Prolonged or incessant mid-range barking with long intervals between barks	When you're left on your own for a long period of time	Hey, is anyone there? I've chewed my toy, licked my bits and explored the kitchen. Now what am I going to do for the next four hours?
Yip-yip-yip sound followed by long drawn-out howl	When you're left on your own and you're absolutely convinced you've been totally forgotten about	Hello … Hello … Remember me?
One or two sharp barks at high or mid-range pitch	When you're pleased to see another dog or your owner	How YOU doin'?
Rapid repetitive barking; low-range pitch	When another person or dog encroaches on your territory	P*** off!
Single sharp, short bark at a lower mid-range pitch	When you're annoyed about something, like being woken from a deep sleep or being petted roughly	WTF!?
Single yelp or very short high-pitched bark	In response to sudden pain	Ouch!

Low-pitched growl-bark	When something has upset or disturbed you and you're ready to get aggressive if it continues	Don't push me, bud!
Undulating growl (pitch rises and falls)	When you're scared but haven't quite made up your mind whether to run or fight	Do you feel lucky? Well do ya, punk?
Series of yelps	When something really scares you	I'm outta here!
Soft whimpering	I'm really frightened	Damn that vacuum cleaner!
Stuttering bark at mid-range pitch	When you want to play	Let's have fun!
Rising bark	When you're enjoying playing	This IS fun!
Sigh	When you decide to settle down for a while	There's only so much satisfaction I can gain from fetching a stick
Excited panting or a howl-yawn	When something you like is about to happen (likely to be going for a walk or eating. Unlikely to be bath time)	Let's do this!
Whining that rises in pitch at the end	When you want or need something	Are we gonna do this or what?
Staccato whimpering in two/three second bursts	When you want to be let in (or out)	Come on! Open the damn door!

BATH TIME

Just as dinner time is the best part of a doggy day, bath time is the worst. Although as a species we tend to take to water, we don't like it when it's contained within a long shiny white porcelain or enamel container that's too smooth to climb out of.

Thankfully, unless you're being regularly entered into dog shows, bath time is infrequent. It is usually triggered by one of the following three situations:

- You're covered in mud
- You've been rolling in fox poop or something that's decomposing
- You start to smell like a wet dog … when you're perfectly dry

On average, you'll probably have a bath about once every four to six weeks. That might not sound a lot, but that's eight to thirteen times a year you'll go through hell.

5 SIGNS THAT BATH TIME IS IMMINENT

1. Your owner will wrap an old towel around you the very instant you come in from a walk.
2. She'll change into old clothes and you know she's not about to work in the garden or start decorating.
3. You'll be lured upstairs with a treat.

4. You're lying on your bed and it's being dragged ever so slowly yet inevitably towards the bathroom door.

5. You'll hear the proclamation, 'Bath time!'

The 5 stages of bath time

Bath time is different for all of us, but it's usually an emotional rollercoaster comprising a number of distinct stages:

Stage 1: Denial

'A bath? No way!' Your first reaction is to refuse to believe that a bath is imminent. It's a normal defence mechanism to protect you from the cold facts (and colder water).

Stage 2: Anger

As the reality sinks in, your emotions change to anger. This is usually directed at your owner, but sometimes it can be targeted at the actual reason for the bath, for example the farmer who owned the field you got muddy in or the decaying pigeon you were compelled to rub against. You'll think things like, 'Damn that bloody fox! If it hadn't pooped in our street

I wouldn't be in this mess. I hope it ends up draped around some rich lady's shoulders.'

Stage 3: Bargaining
You'll appeal to a higher power to try and negotiate your way out of the situation. 'Doggy God, I promise I'll never pull on my leash or eat my poop if you just get me out of this bath.'

Stage 4: Depression
During this stage you'll become saddened by the certainty of being shampooed. You'll probably be quiet and withdrawn and spend the time leading up to the bath mournful and sullen.

Stage 5: Acceptance
'It's going to be okay. I can't fight it so I might as well prepare for it.' In this last stage you'll embrace your inevitable soaking with serene composure. Plus you'll look forward to getting a treat afterwards.

CANINE COMMENT

Sasha Bath time. What you gain in cleanliness, you lose in dignity.

See also *Drying off*

BED

We're fortunate in that we have a much more flexible approach to where we doze than humans. You'll notice that when it comes to sleeping, they have to rely on a special item of furniture in a specific room and they'll fuss about silly things they call mattresses, valances, pillows, blankets and sheets.

In stark contrast, what we choose as a bed is any surface that meets these three criteria:

A. It's soft
B. It's clean
C. It's somewhere your owner wants to sit

BEGGING

Begging should come as naturally to us as chasing cats or licking our genitals. The key thing to remember about begging is that there's absolutely no shame in it. Begging doesn't make you a bad dog or a dog with low self-esteem; it makes you a dog who usually gets what he or she wants.

The urge to seek shelter is programmed into our DNA, so it's perfectly natural to beg to get into your owner's nice warm bedroom, and ultimately, their nice warm bed.

Similarly, begging is the best way to get food. It's a method that falls somewhere between ripping open bin bags left out for collection and having food put in your bowl. Since you're more likely to beg for food than shelter, this section will concentrate on the former scenario.

Good things to beg for	Bad things to beg for
• Food	• Being neutered
• Admittance into a bedroom	• The Cone of Shame
• Forgiveness	• Going outside in the cold
	• Obedience lessons
	• Bath time

10 rules for successfully begging for food

Rule 1: Timing is everything
Try and arrange your sleep patterns so you're awake between midday and 2 p.m., and 6 p.m. and 8 p.m. Nothing's more frustrating than waking up from a long, deep sleep and sauntering into the kitchen only to see the remains of a chicken carcass being dumped unceremoniously into the trash or the smell of gravy-stained plates disappearing into the dishwasher.

Rule 2: Adopt a siege mentality
Approach each mealtime with a 'prepare for the worst' mentality. This attitude means you'll be able to cope with being attacked (i.e. being shouted at) and disappointed (i.e. not getting that sausage).

Rule 3: You don't have to be a puppy to have puppy-dog eyes

Remember the human saying that the eyes are the doors to a nice full belly. If you're the doggy equivalent of Derren Brown, you've got it made. For most of us, though, we can't rely on hypnotizing our owners and instead have to make do with looking as forlorn and pitiful as possible.

Rule 4: Know your whimper from your whine

Whining just puts humans off. They find the high-pitched sound annoying and will try and stop it by throwing you out of the room rather than throwing you food. Whimpering, on the other hand, shows that you're in some sort of distress and, while being peckish isn't quite the same as being injured, they'll respond far more positively to this sound.

Rule 5: Use all the tricks at your disposal

It could be placing a paw on your owner's knee, standing up so you can survey the table top or making a bark that sounds uncannily like 'sausages'. Don't worry about 'selling out' or a complete and utter loss of dignity. Remember, when it comes to begging for food, there is no wrong way.

Rule 6: Be flexible

If all your attempts to secure scraps from owner one fail, be prepared to try your game plan on all the members of the family. You may have seen humans 'working a room'; in this case you have to work the table.

Rule 7: Exploit guests

If there are people seated at the table you've never seen before, choose them as your first targets. There's a good chance that they'll see your pathetic look as cute rather than annoying, and being unaware of mealtime protocol, will probably hand you food before your owner has a chance to intervene. And by intervene, I mean shout and lock you out of the room.

Rule 8: Don't take 'No!' for an answer

Sure, it's not pleasant being shouted at each time you beg, but every time this happens just think what's worse – being called a 'bad dog!' or missing out on that barbecued pork rib. It's a no-brainer.

Rule 9: If it ain't broke …

Your own way to beg might involve resting your chin on your owner's lap or picking your bowl up with your teeth. If you've managed to hit upon a tried-and-tested technique for begging and you know it works, stick with this proven method. It might be tempting to try and improve upon it or enhance it to secure yet more food, but it's best not to take the risk.

Rule 10: Be dogmatic

Sorry for this pun, but begging is often a war of attrition. Your owners will start off the meal with a defiant attitude to treating you to morsels from their plate. The only way to win here is to be equally as determined that you're not going to leave the room without some 'real' food in your stomach. Tenacity and perseverance will often win the day.

THE FIVE-SECOND RULE

If food falls on the floor and no one retrieves it in five seconds, it's perfectly okay for you to eat it. Although, to be honest, this rule probably won't be recognized by your owners. And you definitely won't have the willpower to wait five seconds.

CANINE COMMENT

Lily It didn't take me long to discover that there is no such thing as looking 'too pathetic'.

Romeo With a little practice, you can keep this up for hours.

BIRDS

It's like the doggy god was toying with us when he invented birds. On the one hand, they make the perfect prey: they're small, they make interesting noises to attract us and that hopping thing they do makes them slow on the ground. On the other hand, as soon as you chase them they leap into the air and won't come down.

So why do we chase them? Well, like running after a stick, it's the thrill of the chase rather than the outcome. As long as you realize you have more chance of catching a squirrel than a bird, you won't be too disappointed.

3 things every dog needs to know about birds

1. They can fly
2. You can't
3. An owl is not a cat with wings

BITING

There's a human saying that goes, 'Never bite the hand that feeds you.'

Ignoring this advice will usually result in you being shouted at or possibly smacked. Worse still, it might result in your owner needing medical attention. When I say 'worse still', I really mean that a consequence might be that it temporarily reduces her ability to provide you with dinner.

BLADDERS

Not yours. I'm talking here about human bladders, their most important internal organ. You'll find it at the base of their stomach, and knowing where it is located is important for a dog.

The human bladder performs two functions. The first is the same as yours: storing urine. The second function is far more important: it acts as your owner's alarm clock.

Pressing down on it with your paws, or your whole body weight, will wake them from a deep sleep so they can open the back door and then feed you.

BONE BURYING

When was the last time you buried a bone? When was the last time you saw another dog bury a bone? (Those *Tom and Jerry* cartoons you might have seen on TV don't count.)

The answer to both of these questions is probably 'I can't remember' or 'never'. Hell, we're so domesticated that most of us don't even dig holes anymore, let alone bury stuff.

Thousands of years ago, we used to bury food to hide it and protect it from scavengers; now that our next meal comes from a packet or tin, we don't need to. And when we're given bones by our owners, we can leave them anywhere in the house, safe in the knowledge that because they're usually covered in drool, no one else will pick them up and take them.

That said, if you *do* have a primeval urge to bury a bone, there are two things you'll need:

A. a bone
B. somewhere you can dig a hole

The 5 steps to successful bone burying

Step 1: Find a suitable location
Step 2: Use your front paws and nose to remove a few inches of topsoil and push it to one side
Step 3: Put the bone in the hole
Step 4: Use your front paws and nose to replace the topsoil and pat it down

Step 5: Remember where you've buried it
N.B. Failure to complete Step 5 will lead to considerable frustration

Good places to bury your bone

- Front garden
- Back garden
- Er, that's about it

Bad places to bury your bone

- Anywhere they're excavating dinosaurs or some Iron Age fort
- Anywhere with a sign that features a skull and crossbones and the word 'minefield'
- Anywhere at the Chelsea Flower Show
- Army firing range
- Cemetery

CANINE COMMENT

Rusty Why do I bury bones in the ground? Because I can't bury them in the tree, duh!

BOOTIES

Nothing says you're a pampered pooch or a mollycoddled mutt more than being seen in public wearing colourful waterproof booties. Despite your loudest protestations, no one will believe you're wearing them to protect a paw injury. You'll get the same reaction from both humans and other dogs: less compassion and more derision.

CANINE COMMENT

Mutley My owners said these booties were this season's 'must-have' accessories. They lied.

BUMPING

This is a tried-and-tested non-verbal way to get your owner's attention.

It's easy. To get them to notice you, all you have to do is nudge their arm. This works well if they're trying to read a newspaper or magazine – especially when holding a steaming hot cup of tea or coffee.

BUTT-SNIFFING

If your owner's face were 70 per cent nose, she'd get called 'Beaky', 'Pinocchio' or 'Gérard Depardieu'. When a dog's face is 70 per cent nose, we look normal. Isn't nature wonderful! It's thanks to our large nose and our 220-million plus sensory cells that we have a sense of smell that's up to 100,000 more sensitive than humans. The advantage is that we can smell sausages from about three streets away. The disadvantages are that we can't get at those sausages and anything really whiffy stinks 100,000 times more.

It's this great sense of smell that gives us all the information we need about another dog, and the process by which we gather said information is butt-sniffing. Don't worry about what others (and by others I mean your owners) think about butt–sniffing; it's perfectly normal behaviour – not some doggy deviant act. In human terms it's the equivalent of checking out another dog's Facebook profile.

The scent emitted from the other dog's anal glands tells us its gender, diet, environment and temperament, but the truth is we don't actually have to poke our nose in their butt. In reality, our acute sense of smell means we can pick all this information up with a couple of whiffs from right across the park or from down the road.

The reason for sniffing dogs' butts is simple. It's so you can gross out your owner by licking or kissing them immediately afterwards.

CANINE OBESITY

Unfortunately, one of the consequences of human obesity is canine obesity. Our owners are too fat and lazy to take us for walkies.

Okay … there *is* another reason why dogs are getting fatter – we love second dinners. We might have just eaten, but as soon as humans put food on the table we want it.

Don't feel guilty about it. It's a natural reaction to having to eat the same boring dry food day after day after day.

10 SIGNS YOU MAY BE A FAT FIDO

1. When humans pet you they comment that you're 'well padded'.
2. You only feel comfortable mating with the lights off.
3. Collars with a single 'X' in the size just aren't comfortable anymore.
4. When the vet puts you on the scales you suck in your stomach.
5. You see a squirrel riding on a cat's back just a few feet away … and you have no energy to do anything about it.
6. You're sometimes mistaken for a Saint Bernard.
7. People ask you when your puppies are due … and you've been spayed.
8. You see yourself gaining weight in places you didn't know were possible. A fat tail? Who has that?
9. You can only get your dog coat on by lying on your back.
10. You went for a walk on the beach and passers-by tried to keep you wet and drag you back in to the sea.

CANINE COMMENT

Princess It's all about the bass (-et hound).

See also *Exercise*

CARS

There's only one thing dogs need to know about cars: four legs good; four wheels bad.

No matter what you hear, it's not fun travelling in motorized transport. There's a romantic notion about dogs travelling with their owners in cars – the lure of the open road, the chance to poke your head out of the window, the wind in your fur and a never-ending series of varied, exciting smells wafting by, while a mysterious destination awaits …

As you probably already know, the reality is somewhat different. Despite all attempts to secure you, you'll be thrown around, jerked this way and that and bumped up and down without any warning. And there's a good chance you'll be sick. When that happens, not only will you still be uncomfortable, but you'll be uncomfortable in a car that now smells of sick. And although a car can whisk you to a truly magical destination, the reality will usually be a disappointment.

The truth about car journeys

Where you think you're going	Where you invariably end up
Park	Vet
Countryside	Vet
Woods	Vet
Beach	Vet
Dog show	Vet
Vet	Kennels

Riding in a car: The dos and don'ts

- DON'T suddenly bark as loud as you can just inches behind your owner's head. The shock could cause your owner to have an accident, and while temporarily being without a car will benefit you, you'll inevitably (and completely unfairly) get blamed for the crash
- DO whimper continually. This should start as soon as you're placed in the car and increase in pitch, timbre and volume until the level of distress you're exhibiting brings the journey to a premature conclusion
- DO drool when sticking your head out of an open window. The wind will catch this and fling it over the windscreen of the following car. You'll find this funny although the driver behind will not
- DON'T view an open sunroof as a challenge. Appreciate it for the cooling air wafting around you, not as an escape opportunity that, while being dramatic, will probably result in injury

- DO let your owners take a photo of you with your paws perched on the steering wheel. Humans find hilarity in this, especially when they post the photo on Facebook with a caption saying, 'It was his turn to drive!' or alluding to their car being a Range Rover. Let them have their fun, and reap the rewards of their good mood later

CANINE COMMENT

Bruno I went for a ride in a car. When we left the house I had testicles. When we returned I didn't. I don't like cars.

Spike Does it look like I'm enjoying this? Well, does it?

CATS

As Sun Tzu remarked, 'To know your enemy, you must become your enemy.' He didn't mean pooping in a box filled with gravel, cruelly toying with injured birds or eating fish heads (well, at least he didn't in my translated doggy edition). What I'm sure he meant was that as dogs, we need to understand cats so we're not surprised by anything they do. However, since a dog's life is a busy life (when we're not sleeping), I've listed the following feline facts to save you the time and embarrassment of finding out for yourself.

Feline facts: 10 things every dog needs to know about cats

- No matter how confident you are, like even if your name is Starey or Mr Staresworthy, don't bother getting into a staring contest with a cat. There will only ever be one winner
- There is only one thing that cats hate more than plants. Dogs
- No matter what tricks you can do, even if it's walking upright on two legs or balancing a dinner plate on your nose, a cat will always, always, ALWAYS win at being cuter
- Unbelievable as it might seem, cats sleep even longer than we do
- Being bitten by a cat WON'T turn you into a cat (but it might hurt)
- Cats are creepy, weird and 'otherworldly'. Is it any wonder that they're associated with witches and Halloween?
- When a cat arches its back it is a sign it's being threatened and is about to attack. It is not an open invitation for you to try and run underneath it
- Cats are always looking for things on which to

sharpen their claws. This can include tree trunks, furniture, scratching posts, or you. Be wary

- They can squeeze into places that you can only dream about, so don't try and emulate them
- They can get away with murder. For example, a cat jumping on the table to eat the remains of a chicken dinner is 'cute.' If you try it, it's 'dirty'

If you hear your owner say, 'It's raining cats and dogs,' don't get overly excited or anxious. He is lying.

CANINE COMMENT

Lexi You see what she's doing? And you're just going to stand there and take a photo?

CESAR MILLAN

If you see your owner with a book or a DVD by this man, be afraid. Be very afraid.

He is known as the Dog Whisperer, but most of us know

him as the Dog Shouty Man. His training techniques have been called controversial and are based on the fact that we should be treated like dogs and that our owners should act like pack leaders, not playmates. Where's the fun in that? He calls this the dominance theory. We call it plain wrong.

If we wanted to be put in our place constantly, yelled at and made to understand rules, boundaries and limitations, we wouldn't be dogs, we'd be children.

CHASING

Chasing stuff is not only instinctive, it's also fun and **so easy** to do!

HOW TO CHASE SOMETHING

1. Run after something really fast.
2. That's it.

What's more, there's absolutely NO pressure. You don't even have to catch up with whatever it is you're running after; the thrill is the chase itself.

Good things to chase

- Balls
- Sticks
- Cats
- Frisbees
- Smaller dogs
- Birds
- Squirrels
- People

Bad things to chase

- Anything stationary
- Bigger dogs
- Cars (they are not metal dogs)
- Your tail (you'll get a headache)

CHEWING

Chewing non-edible objects is an instinct over which we have absolutely no control.

Apart from puppies, who chew to ease the pain of teething, the rest of us chew because we're anxious, lonely, bored or just want attention – and whatever the reason, we don't discriminate about what we put in our mouths. When the urge comes, we chew the nearest available object to us, whatever it may be. It's as simple as that.

Ha, you didn't seriously believe that, did you?

Of course we decide what to chew and what not to chew! I mean, that's half the fun, isn't it?

It's a decision based on this long-established formula, where *GL* is gratification level, *D* the duration of the chew, N^2 is naughtiness and *ch* is choking hazard.

$$GL = \frac{D \times N^2}{ch}$$

For example, faced with a remote control or an old blanket, of course you'd go for the remote control. Likewise, if you see your owner's brand-new expensive shoes and a cushion within reach, it's a no-brainer!

In most households there is a huge range of chewable objects, each with their own merits.

My guide to chewable objects

Remote controls
Pros: Satisfying crunchy sound; the knowledge that until it's replaced you'll be saved from overexposure to bad TV.
Cons: You might swallow parts of it by mistake. Small plastic buttons are relatively harmless. Alkaline batteries are not.

Papers
Pros: Pleasing ripping sound; the sight of your saliva making ink run; the chance that what you rip up might

be something really important and irreplaceable, like a handwritten treasure map or a breakthrough scientific formula.

Cons: Paper is so chewable, any gratification is sadly over too soon.

Wallets

Pros: The texture and smell of leather; the satisfying crunch of credit cards; the taste of paper money. What's not to like?

Cons: A high likelihood that you'll hear the words 'Bad Dog!' shouted louder than you have ever heard them shouted before.

Mobile phones

Pros: None really … unless you like the taste of glass.

Cons: The taste of glass.

Books

Pros: Old books have a nice musty smell that can be enjoyed while you rip the covers off and start on the pages.

Cons: Possible paper cuts.

Cushions

Pros: We can't eat chocolate, but this is the home-furnishing equivalent. Once you get through the difficult exterior a surprise awaits – a soft filling.

Cons: Really messy. Difficult to hide the evidence.

CANINE COMMENT

Archie It was like this when I got here ...

See also *Shoes*

CHRISTMAS

This is a festive period that seems to occur at the coldest time of the human year, every year. You'll recognize it by a strange indoor tree, lots more people in your house and a dangerous increase in your owners' stress levels.

During this period you'll notice your owners get up later and spend more time napping on the sofa, the TV programmes will be louder and brighter than normal and walkies might be at a different time to when you're used to (or worse, cancelled at short notice).

As you're aware, dogs thrive on structure, so these changes to your routine during this season will probably be disconcerting. However, despite this, there are two words that can make Christmas worth looking forward to: buffet table.

In order to enjoy (or at least tolerate) this time of year, it's best to stick to some tried-and-tested festive rules.

A canine Christmas:
The 10 commandments

1. Your territory will be invaded by large numbers of people you rarely see. Your owners will call them guests. To you they're intruders. Treat them accordingly.
2. The tree that appears in the living room is part of a strange human ritual. Peeing against it will be seen as blasphemy.

3. There will be a thin wire connecting the lights on the tree to the wall. Don't chew this, or you will regret the consequences.
4. Despite what you think, if you eat Christmas decorations you will not poop gold tinsel.
5. There will be many brightly coloured packages under the tree. One of them is probably for you. It's not your fault you can't read, so rip open all of them until you find it.
6. A fat man in a red suit and with a white beard might appear in your house one night. This is probably your owner rather than a burglar. Don't be scared. Oh yes, and don't bite him.

7. A mince pie and glass of milk will usually be left in the lounge this same night. If this is within reach, it's fair game.

8. The wooden figures in the nativity scene make perfect chew toys. (N.B. The baby Jesus is very small. If you swallow him, the Second Coming might be quite painful.)

9. Your owners will feel the need to attach fake reindeer antlers to your head. Shake these off a split second before they try and take a photograph.

10. There will be a large dinner with an excess of guests and an even greater excess of food. Beg like you've never begged before.

CANINE COMMENT

Crosby Ho, ho, ho? I don't think so.

CIRCLING BEFORE BEDTIME

This might be a great source of amusement to our owners, but the truth is we can't help it. Years and years ago when we lived in the wild, we'd spin in circles before lying down in order to flatten the grass and scare aware any pests hiding there. Today, even though we sleep on warm rugs, plush lined doggy baskets or the owner's king-sized bed, we go through this inherited routine by pure instinct.

As demonstrated by the number of times we've ended up on YouTube videos, humans find this hilarious.

Just humour them.

COLLARS

There seems to be as wide a choice of collars as there are breeds. Most of you will have leather or fabric collars of various colours and styles from the simple to the pretentious. From spots and stripes to Liberty prints and the old clichés, paw prints or bones, there are some looks that not all breeds can pull off.

What's in and what's so last season

Flea collars

They might be small and discreet, but a flea collar says more about your diminished social status than itching ever does. It's like a human wearing a replica football shirt.

Spiked or studded leather collars
This macho look is something that younger dogs tend to carry off more effectively. In human terms, older dogs wearing this type of collar look less 'biker gang' and more S&M aficionado.

Leopard-print collars
When it comes to collars, faux fur is a fashion faux pas.

Crystal diamanté
ONLY to be worn if you meet one of these conditions:
A. Your owner can carry you under one arm without later requiring the services of a chiropractor
B. Your usual mode of transportation is a handbag
C. You're a cat

Pirate
Collars with a skull and crossbones motif are only permitted if your owner has a peg leg or a parrot called Polly.

Pimped and personalized
Leather collars (various shades) featuring your name in diamanté and chrome letters. The criteria for being able to carry this look off is whether your name is a) short (usually fewer than eight letters) and b) suitable. Ask yourself, does my name look good spelled out in costume jewellery?
If you're called something like Killer or Rambo then the answer is probably no.

Collars featuring bow ties
Really? REALLY?

SPECIALIZED COLLARS TO AVOID AT ALL TIMES

Shock collars

Ignore a command and this type of collar will vibrate or, if you're really unlucky, deliver a small shock. Owners will call it 'aversive training'. You will say, 'That bloody hurts!'

Choke Chain

Nothing with the word 'choke' in its name can be good – and such is the case with these collars, which tighten when you pull on your leash. They're meant to train you to respond to commands but all they'll do is make you angry and resentful. If you're unfortunate enough to have a choke chain, make your owner feel guilty and unnerved by faking strangulation at every opportunity. Yelp, make a gurgling sound and play dead. Your owner will soon realize he made the wrong collar choice.

Harnesses

Technically not collars, although they have the same function. If you tend to pull a lot you might end up wearing one of these. They avoid pressure on your neck but they make you resemble a guide dog wannabe. Not a good look.

CANINE COMMENT

Honey Pie I'm not just an alpha male. I'm a bad boy …

COMPUTERS

Computers are your enemy. Not in a *Terminator*/Skynet global domination way, though. I'm talking about the fact that more than other people or even other pets, these devices are the things that most compete for our attention at home.

How do you identify a computer? Well, it looks like a small television and it's the contraption your owner spends hours each day sitting in front of, laughing at endless videos of dogs – dogs bouncing on trampolines, dogs overwhelmed with tennis balls, dogs trying to bring a wide stick through a narrow gap or dogs saying what sounds like 'hello'.

And every minute they spend looking at these videos of dogs is a minute they could be playing with their real-life dog.

And that, my friend, is what humans call irony.

5 REASONS WHY DOGS WILL NEVER EVER USE COMPUTERS

1. A mouse has more appeal as a chew toy than a device for controlling a graphical user interface.
2. Old habits die hard: we'd mark each website by trying to pee on the screen rather than clicking on 'bookmark this page'.
3. The commands 'heel', 'sit' and 'stay' are fair enough, but Ctrl-Alt-Delete?
4. A drool-covered keyboard is difficult to use.
5. Carpal paw syndrome.

CANINE COMMENT

Buster I got really annoyed when I discovered I couldn't stick my head out of Windows 8.1.

COSTUMES

You may think it's bad enough to be led around on a collar and have commands shouted at you, but owners take humiliation to a whole new level when they decide to dress us up in ridiculous costumes and then share these images across this social media thing.

Maybe they find the sight of us in these stupid clothes amusing, entertaining or even alluring (let's all hope it's not the latter). It's difficult to know the reasons, but the fact is that during your life you will have at least one of these degrading experiences, usually at Christmas or Halloween. What's even more humiliating than being forced to wear these outfits is the fact that your owner will have invariably got the size wrong and the costume will be too small. Not only will this restrict your movement, but far worse than any shame you might suffer is the fact that you'll look chubby.

Since forearmed (or forepawed) is forewarned, I've prepared this list of what fancy dress ideas you might be made to endure before you're able to shake them off or wriggle your way to freedom.

Reindeer antlers
Not strictly a costume as such, this is more an accessory that clips on to your head and makes it look like Doctor Frankenstein was busy with you and Rudolph.

Easter bunny ears
As above, but more disturbing. This ensemble can make you

look like you're in some canine version of the Playboy Club.

Santa costume
Sometimes you may get off lightly and only have a Santa hat plonked on your head, which can be removed with a brisk shake. In most cases, though, you'll be subjected to the full Santa costume, which will probably include a hood. Your owners will then try and force you to pose for photos in front of the Christmas tree. Displaying an interest in eating the presents will soon curtail their attempts.

Christmas elf
Very demeaning. Green felt is so 1980s.

Superman
Is it a bird? Is it a plane? No, it's you in a cheap, nasty acrylic cape that is also a fire hazard. The good thing about this costume is that you won't need a superpower to take it off. Repeated pawing at the strings securing it around your neck will remove it quicker than you can say 'Kryptonite'.

Male stripper

Just as there's no way to make these two words seem anything less than unsavoury, the costume itself has the exact same effect. Be prepared to wear a bow tie and little white shirt cuffs on your front legs. The whole stripper idea is especially weird – what can a dog strip down to? Doesn't your owner realize you're already naked?!

Tiger/Leopard/Lion/Zebra etc.

Wearing a onesie in public is embarrassing enough. Wearing an animal print one that makes you look like you live in the jungle or on the veld is worse. And no matter how hard it tries, a pug with a fake Velcro mane will never ever be able to pull off a convincing King of Beasts look.

Rasta dog

Wear this and not only will you look ridiculous, but you'll also stereotype a whole spiritual movement at a single stroke. There's only one advantage of looking like Bob Marley and Me: it's easy to shake off the Rasta cap and dreads and use it to poop in.

Marilyn Monroe

A dog in a skimpy white dress wearing fake human breasts? I hope you have the RSPCA on speed dial.

Hot dog

Dachshunds have enough body-image problems, so why would owners want to attach a fake bun to their dog's sides and fake relish to their backs? This isn't humiliation; it's a hate crime.

COSTUMES THAT HANG DOWN AT THE FRONT TO MAKE IT LOOK LIKE YOU'RE STANDING ON TWO LEGS

Increasingly popular for smaller dogs, with these costumes you're forced to insert your front paws into the 'legs' while fake arms protrude from the side to make it look like you're a small person with a dog's head. Whether your owner wants you to resemble Elvis, Yoda, a pirate, Michael Jackson or Dracula, the impression these outfits actually give is that you've eaten the intended subject and have draped their lifeless body around your neck.

CANINE COMMENT

Henry Kill me now.

CANINE COMMENT

Rebel There is so much wrong with my costume I just don't know where to start.

See also *Fashion*

CROTCH-SNIFFING

Did Atlantis exist, who was Jack the Ripper and what's the truth about the Bermuda Triangle?

These are apparently some of the greatest human mysteries of all time, but far more enigmatic is the truth behind why we sniff human crotches.

For hundreds of years man has pondered over this mystery and they believe we do it as a greeting and/or a way to gather information.

Really? With all the hundreds of other things in the world to sniff, do you really think we'd choose human groins over something far more appealing, like decomposing food or another dog's urine?

No. The reason you should sniff a human crotch is because it makes them feel extremely awkward.

When to crotch-sniff

Do it when the human has company, particularly if they're with a date, their boss or a religious leader. Your objective should be to cause maximum embarrassment so that the other person automatically has one of these thoughts about the human being sniffed:

1. 'Hmmmm. He's more than man's best friend. I must call the RSPCA.'
2. 'I wonder if he's packing illegal substances in his underpants.'
3. 'I bet he hasn't washed down there for days.'
4. 'I know he said he loves his dog, but really!'

DECODING SECRET CONVERSATIONS

Sometimes your owners will use code words for certain things in the mistaken belief that we won't have any idea what they're talking about, and that to decipher them we'd need the canine equivalent of the Enigma machine. How wrong they are …

The code owners use	What they really mean
W.A.L.K.	Walk
W.A.L.K.I.E.S.	Walkies
D.I.N.N.E.R.T.I.M.E.	Dinner time
P.A.R.K.	Park
V.E.T.	Vet

DINNER TIME

Better than walkies, better than fetch and definitely better than chasing something, dinner time is the highlight of the doggy day.

In fact, there's only one thing better than dinner time, and that's two dinner times – when an owner feeds you again without realizing.

It won't be long before your body clock (your stomach) will know when it's dinner time, probably to within plus or minus two minutes. In dog terms this is similar to the accuracy of an atomic clock.

Most dogs have their own bowl; however, if you share your home with one or more dogs your owner may try to train you and the others to come to your bowls individually when called. I have one thing to say to these humans: good luck.

N.B. Some owners will call both the meal they give you at the start of the day and the meal they give you at the end of the day 'dinner time'. Go figure.

CANINE COMMENT

Bandit I'm hungry. Do I need to be any more obvious?

DOGGY CAMS

Insidious devices that would have given animal champion George Orwell apoplexy, these miniature cameras, sometimes containing microphones, are placed strategically around the house by your owners so they can keep an eye on you when they're out – mainly in the mistaken belief (or rather, hope) that they'll log in one day and see you wearing clothes and prancing around on two legs.

Doggy cams are usually located just out of reach on a high shelf or mantelpiece, pointing towards the sofa, our basket or a favourite chair. The best way to deal with them, therefore, is not to avoid them, but rather to exploit them by making sure you act up when the camera light glows.

How to worry your owners when you know you're on camera

1. Hold your breath so it looks like you've died.
2. Cock your leg so it looks like you're peeing.
3. Face away from the camera and dry retch. Do this repeatedly.
4. Pretend you've just pooped by booty-scooting along the carpet left to right, then when you're out of the camera's field of vision, come scooting back into frame. Repeat three or four times.
5. Howl, not like a wolf-in-the-wild, but like a pained, wounded dog who really, really hates and resents his owners for abandoning him.

CANINE COMMENT

Snowy What you get up to when your owners are out is your business. Stay out of camera range to preserve your mystery.

DOG PSYCHOLOGISTS

You may have heard your owners talking about taking you to the dog shrink. Don't worry, you're not going to some place where you go in as a German Shepherd and come out as a miniature poodle.

What they're talking about is a dog psychologist. This is someone whose job entails conning your owners out of a large sum of money in order to identify the reasons for any so-called behavioural issues. All that will happen is that they'll observe you playing and interacting and decide that the reason you poop on the carpet is because your mother didn't lick you enough as a puppy.

CANINE COMMENT

Brunhilda I was ready for my psychoanalysis. Next thing, I'm being told NOT to sit on the couch … Talk about mixed messages! No wonder I have issues.

DOG SHOWS

Your owners may think you're the prettiest pooch or the handsomest hound and might bestow that accolade on you with alarming regularity, but, honestly, it counts for nothing.

To be recognized for any outstanding achievement you need to be judged independently – and that means entering a dog show. Be warned, though, you don't just need a glossy coat; you need a thick skin. And just like human beauty contests, you can be surrounded by some real bitches.

The motivation to win a dog show isn't to please your owner. (In fact, there's great satisfaction to be gained from their reaction when you fail to win – it's not just German shepherds, Dachshunds, Rottweilers, Weimaraners and Dobermans that experience schadenfreude, after all.) No, the incentives to succeed are respect, a shiny cup and a medal, but most of all the chance to look at your fellow competitors with an expression that says, 'In your face!'

There are essentially two types of dog show: professional and amateur.

CANINE COMMENT

Oscar Winners never quit and quitters never win. I like to eat poop.

3 signs of a professional dog show

1. The judges all look like they were caught in a tweed factory explosion
2. You won't win if you behave like a dog (i.e. barking, wagging your tail or smiling)
3. Before and during the show your owners will be as highly strung as miniature poodles. And just as snappy

3 signs of an amateur dog show

1. Categories include 'Best Puppy-Dog Eyes' and 'Waggiest Tail'
2. If you poop in the ring people will laugh, not gasp
3. Not having testicles isn't seen as a handicap (well, not as far as the judges go)

10 tips for dog show success

1. Don't look at the judges' crotches thinking, 'I wonder if I should sniff that, just to embarrass them'; look straight in their eyes.
2. Hold your head high and pretend that you've already won. It might sound corny (crazy, even) but tell yourself over and over again, 'I AM the rosette! I AM the rosette!'
3. Take comfort in the fact that your owner will be more nervous than you (especially if she's worried that you're suddenly going to lick your balls without warning).
4. Make sure you poop or pee before the show. You'll really thank me for this advice.
5. Always maintain excellent posture. Shoulders back, jaw parallel to the ground, and back straight – but most importantly, walk with that sassy attitude!
6. Get plenty of sleep the day before. That means eighteen hours, not the usual twelve to fourteen.
7. Never get yourself down because you think that Hungarian vizsla looks overly confident or that

Pomeranian looks far too cute. It's easy to be overly critical of yourself (Shar Peis, you know what I'm talking about).

8. Go steady on the treats. If you're in good shape, you'll be more confident.

9. Make sure you're ready to go into the ring (in other words, you're not napping or chasing something). When it comes to dog shows there is no such thing as being fashionably late.

10. Be on your best behaviour at all times. If a judge or another dog annoys you (face it, it's a dog show, it's going to happen), turn the other cheek. There'll be plenty of time to bite them after you've won.

CANINE COMMENT

Suki Okay, it might not be Crufts, but winning that Julia Roberts lookalike contest was good enough for me.

DOG WHISTLES

Humans think they're so clever, inventing a training device that emits sound in the ultrasonic range so only we can hear it. If you haven't experienced one, count yourself lucky. This sound is probably the most annoying and irritating noise you'll ever hear (apart from the latest Little Mix single).

CANINE COMMENT

Oscar La la la la. I'm not listening!

DOG YOGA

Hessian shopping bags, children with names such as Jocasta and Artemis and cheeses no one has ever heard of … Look, I'm not generalizing or being prejudiced, but if you observe these sorts of things where you live then there's a good chance that your owner is the type of person who will enrol you in dog yoga classes (or 'doga', as they cringingly refer to it).

It started in the US as a way for guilty health-conscious owners to spend more time with their pets. But us dogs simply want to go for walkies, not get involved in a spiritual discipline. Despite what you might have heard, doga will *not* help you relax.

Being lifted into unnatural poses or being positioned into some weird stance will just make you feel very self-conscious and stressed out. And as for your owner's claim that it will nurture 'your canine spiritual wellbeing', well, that's just barking!

There is only ever one reason owners take their dogs to dog yoga. That's to tell other people that they take their dogs to dog yoga.

CANINE COMMENT

Mimi They said I would enter a Zen-like state. Instead I peed on the mat.

DROOL

Drool, or as it's known in doggy circles, 'liquid gold', is a substance with multiple uses. Sure, the enzymes and chemicals help break up our food and aid digestion, neutralize acids, aid in taste detection, create a protective layer for our teeth, destroy bacteria and assist in the healing process of any wounds, but the main function of drool is as a way of marking your possessions to prevent your owners moving or interfering with them.

DRYING OFF

The only upside to having a bath (and believe me, there *is* only one upside) is the opportunity to dry yourself afterwards. And by dry yourself, I mean shake water all over the bathroom and your owner in equal measure.

How to shake yourself dry

Look. You're a dog with millions of years of evolution. Don't insult me by saying you're not sure what to do.

Shaking, of course, isn't confined to bath time. It can be used to catastrophic effect any time you're wet, whether it's from the rain or from jumping in a river, the sea or a lake. In these instances you can turn it into a fun game where you score points based on who you soak, attempting to break your personal record each time you splash.

Who you shake water all over	Points scored
Your owner	5
A complete stranger	10*
A couple	15*
Family having a picnic	20*
A bride in her wedding dress	30*
Anyone sunbathing	40*

* Add 5 points if they get really shouty with your owner

See also *Bath Time* and *Swimming*

EATING POOP

There's only one thing you need to know about this habit …
Just because we can, doesn't mean that we should.

ELIZABETHAN COLLARS

The name sounds classy, almost majestic and noble, but no
matter how humans dress it up, this plastic device, attached
to your normal collar, is still recognized by dogs the world
over as the Cone of Shame.

Advantages: It'll prevent you scratching or licking a wound or infection.
Disadvantages: You'll look like a doggy dork.
Summary: When your ability to lick your own genitals is taken away, you'll be surprised how much free time you have.

How to maintain any semblance of self-esteem when wearing the Cone of Shame

I'm really sorry, but there's really no way to maintain dignity by styling out what is in effect an upturned plastic lampshade. Sure, you may think that you can convince other dogs that it's a special device to gather sound waves so you can hear from even further away, that it's a handy way of carrying toys and snacks from room to room or even that you're waiting for it to be filled with treats … but the thing is, no one will believe you. Ever.

CANINE COMMENT

Carlos Sure. It's funny when someone else is wearing it.

EXERCISE

When it comes to exercise, how much is 'enough' depends on your age, breed and health. A ten-month-old Jack Russell is going to need a lot more exercise than a ten-year-old Labrador, while basset hounds of any age are content to slob around the house most of the time.

Most exercise takes the form of walks on the leash around your local area or, if you're lucky, being allowed off the leash in parks, fields, woods or along a beach. If you're unlucky, however, your owner will involve you in his or her own exercises like jogging, rollerblading or cycling. Surprisingly, this can occasionally be fun too – if only for the carnage you can create by running right across their path without warning.

But you don't just have to do strenuous exercise to keep fit. It's amazing how many calories you can burn each time you carry out mundane tasks that you probably take for granted.

Keeping fit without really trying

Everyday task	Calories burned
Chasing your tail	16
Chasing a bird or squirrel	20
Running up and down the hallway when the doorbell goes	22
Rolling in something you really shouldn't	9
Running away when your owner catches you rolling in something you shouldn't	15

Barging through the front door before your owner	6
Stealing socks out of the washing basket and hiding them in the house	8
Following your owner around the house for no particular reason	21
Jumping up on the sofa	8
Jumping down from the sofa	5
Annoyingly pawing at the newspaper or magazine while your owner is trying to read	4
Chewing shoes	10
Hiding shoes	14
Booty scoot (per metre)	6
Pawing open a black bin bag and scavenging its contents	4
Licking your genitalia while owner is eating	3
Frantically trying to escape from the bath	19
Running away from the vacuum cleaner	11
Shedding fur	1

CANINE COMMENT

Austin I'm taking regular exercise. Today I rolled to the right; tomorrow I'll roll to the left.

CANINE COMMENT

Petey Feel the burn? I don't think so.

See also *Canine obesity*

FASHION
(Or does this dog coat make me look fat?)

It's a moot point why we need coats. Firstly, we have fur, which is quite waterproof, thank you very much, and keeps us warm. Secondly, the rain and cold tend to discourage our owners from taking us out anyway.

However, if you do find yourself forced into a dog coat, the important thing to remember is that the reason is not because your owner wants to protect you from the elements; it's to make you their fashion accessory.

My guide to dog coats

Tartan
Only to be worn if you're one of these breeds: Scottie, Skye terrier, Cairn terrier, West Highland terrier or Shetland sheepdog. The jury's still out when it comes to Border collies.

Camouflage
There are only three reasons that justify you wearing a camo-coat: a) you're a military mascot, b) you're a bomb-sniffing dog, c) your owner is a bit weird.

Fleece dog jumpers
Technically not coats, these warm roll-neck jumpers cover your torso and front paws, extending as far as your tail. To be avoided by Rottweilers, Dobermans and Weimaraners because you'll look less like a dog and more like a U-Boat commander.

Anything with vertical stripes
Pugs, Pomeranians, chihuahuas, Shih Tzus, Pekinese: wear this type of coat and you'll instantly look taller.

Black PVC
Thought by many owners to be the epitome of style, these tend to look less like a fashion statement (a good one, at least) and more like you've become tangled up in a bin bag. Running away is preferable to wearing one of these abominations.

Coats that resemble tuxedos

These feature white 'shirts' and bow ties (see page 52) and are marketed to vacuous owners as dog coats for special occasions. This sounds quite appealing until you realize that it's highly improbable that you'll be invited to a party at an ambassador's residence or to a gala political fundraiser.

Leather

Why do owners really think it's acceptable to dress their dog up as an extra from *The Matrix*? A quick walk down the road is likely to lead to a feeling of embarrassment rather than empowerment.

Explorer-type coats

If Bear Grylls or other wilderness survival experts were dogs, they'd wear one of these. They're fleece-lined, completely waterproof and provide almost total cover from the wet, cold, wind and frost and usually have names like 'Stormguard', 'Everest' or something that includes the word 'Ultimate'. While they do offer protection for long walks in remote, exposed and hostile areas, you'll look like some kind of doggy dipstick wearing one while tied up outside Tesco.

CANINE COMMENT

Lucky When you look at what my owners make me wear, you can appreciate the irony in my name.

See also *Costumes, undignified*

FETCH

When you're a new pup this seems like the best game in the whole world. It's easy to understand and you can burn off loads of excess energy. As you get older, however, you realize the futility of it all, and what was once an entertaining diversion is now a lacklustre chore.

Yet, whatever stage of life you're at, it's important to understand that there are two versions of fetch, each with established rules depending on whether you're a human or a dog.

How to play fetch

The players
The game of fetch involves two players: one human and one dog.

The equipment
This consists of 'the object' – usually a ball or a stick, but could also be a Frisbee. Do not under any circumstance be tricked into playing with a boomerang.

The playing arena
Any open space, but typically a back garden, park, meadow, field or beach.

Duration of play

Unlike most sports, there is no set time limit. Fetch ends when you or your owner gets bored. In most cases you will experience this feeling first.

Fake throws

While there's nothing to prevent owners doing this, the ploy is considered extremely unsportsmanlike. If your owner gains any sort of satisfaction as a result of successfully tricking a dog, feel sorry for them. They have issues.

The 2 versions of fetch

Your owner's

1. He throws the object
2. You run after it
3. You pick it up in your mouth
4. You bring it back to him
5. Repeat steps 1 to 4

Yours

1. Your owner throws the object
2. You run after it
3. You pick it up in your mouth
4. You sit there and drop it
5. Your owner shouts 'Fetch!' repeatedly, with gradually

increasing volume each time
6. You ignore him
7. You continue to sit where the object landed or run off in a random direction without it
8. Your owner sighs, then reluctantly trudges towards where the object is and picks it up
9. Repeat steps 1 to 8

BEWARE OF THE SNOWBALL

In winter, your owner might throw snowballs for you to fetch and take great delight in your confusion and frustration when trying to retrieve something that disintegrates on impact. Do not fall for this mean trick.

See also *Ball throwers* and *Frisbee-catching*

FIREWORKS

According to a study I've conducted with my pals, the five sounds that cause the greatest distress in dogs are fireworks, Michael Bublé records, thunder, doorbells and vacuum cleaners – in that order.

If you haven't experienced fireworks yet then consider yourself lucky. They're small, man-made explosive devices that create noise, light and smoke. But especially noise. Humans use them to celebrate events like their New Year, religious festivals or something they call Guy Fawkes Night. Some dog behaviourists suggest that your owner should familiarize you with fireworks by playing you a sound-effect CD, slowly increasing the volume until you become used to the loud bangs. This could have two effects. It could acclimatize you to the noise or it could traumatize you even more.

Don't risk the outcome. If you think your owner looks like he's going to try this experiment, chew the CD.

Dos and don'ts for fireworks nights

- DON'T go in the garden when fireworks are going off. This is not the time to prove your bravery
- DO have dinner before you expect the disturbances to start because once the fireworks begin you may be too anxious to eat*
- DON'T beg your owner to take you to a fireworks display. This sort of behaviour is what humans call 'reckless'
- DO try and convince your owner to turn on the TV as this will help to mask the noise of the fireworks. On these nights you should be thankful for the loud, screechy talent shows that pass for man's light entertainment
- DO take refuge anywhere that makes you feel safe.

Whether you're a Dachshund or a Doberman, there's no shame in cowering under furniture
- DON'T bark at the fireworks. They cannot hear you and are not scared of you

*I know this sounds far-fetched, but it could happen.

See also *Thunderstorms*

FLEAS, LICE, MITES AND TICKS

Dogs get a raw deal when it comes to one creature acting as host for another. Rhinos have tick-birds and sharks have remora fish to clean their teeth and eat dead skin; the connection between the different species is gratifying, harmonious and mutually beneficial.

We have fleas, lice, mites and ticks. Not so much a symbiotic relationship … more a bloody nuisance.

My guide to parasites

Fleas

While the symptoms are bad (severe itching, scratching or biting of infected areas), what's actually worse are two specific treatments you may have to suffer. Count yourself lucky if your owner only uses drops, powder or a spray. Sometimes, though, they go down the 'regular bath' route, which can be more irritating than the parasites themselves. Even worse than that is the flea collar, a device guaranteed to kill two things stone dead: the parasites and your reputation.

Lice

While not as prevalent as fleas, suffering from lice is still a social stigma worse than being seen eating poop. Worse, even, than being seen eating poop that's not your own. Having a lice infestation can make you go bald, and treatment might include having your fur shaved around the infested areas, which is never a good look. Humans believe that baldness can be attractive or that it's a sign of virility, but that's never the case with dogs. I mean, have you seen a Mexican hairless?

Mites

Having mites makes you wish you had fleas. They're everything you don't want a parasite to be: too small to be seen by your owner's naked eye, clawed, they lay eggs under the skin and are highly contagious. A parasite with just one of these characteristics is bad enough; mites have all four. You're probably itching just reading this.

Ticks

You can get ticks if you spend lots of time walking in long grass. They're like big mites and are known as the vampires of parasites. They burrow into your skin in the areas where you're least hairy. This means your face and neck, the insides of your legs and around your 'special place'. But apart from the danger of infection and disease, there's a far greater risk – and that's from your owners trying to remove them in a variety of ways that they think will work, but don't. These include covering them in nail varnish remover, butter, paraffin, or worse – by burning them off.

Remember, if your owner holds a match or cigarette anywhere near your fur, run. As fast as you can. Being burned anywhere, particularly if it's near your undercarriage, will be far more painful than anything a tick can do.

FOOD

If you have an opportunity to eat sausages, followed by cake, followed by spaghetti in a rich pasta sauce, that's okay. Humans would not approve of this combination, but as a dog you don't need to get precious about the whole sweet/savoury thing. There's only one thing you need to know: **food is food is food.**

FOUL SMELLS, ROLLING IN

You're happily trotting down the street, taking in the fresh air and enjoying the sunshine on your fur when you pick up the unmistakable scent of fox poop. Suddenly your genetic programming kicks in and you're overcome with an irresistible urge: must … roll … in it. Got to … roll … in it …

Although deep down we know it's going to result in two things – being shouted at and a bath – we still do it. This ingrained habit goes back to the olden days when we were all wild. It was a way to hide our doggy smell as we stealthily crept up on our prey. It worked surprisingly well and it's a trait that continues today, even though the nearest we get to hunting is to sidle up to a tin of Pedigree chicken and gravy.

The following is a guide to some of the best smells that take us back to our doggy roots:

Fox poop
The napalm of foul smells. I don't mean it sets you on fire, but not only does it have a sickly smell, it really clings to your fur. So hard to remove, yet so satisfying.

Cowpats and horse manure
You're unlikely to come across these in towns, but a walk in the countryside can often reach a satisfying conclusion – sticky with the comforting odour of the farm or stables.

Animal remains
This might be a dead bird, fox, mouse, rat, cat or squirrel

by the roadside, or a seagull on the beach. If you're lucky it might already be decomposing or, as we say, 'ripe'.

Old food
Foxes have a knack of knocking over food bins in the night and scavenging among the remains. Sometimes they leave something for you to roll in. The most sought-after remains include stale pasta and tomato sauce and rancid chicken.

Vomit
Don't be too choosy. It could come from a cat, a dog or a human. Having your owner take you for walkies near a pub car park will often provide a good source of the latter.

CANINE COMMENT

Charlie Mmmmm. Fox poop. The Chanel No.5 of foul smells.

FOXES

Just because all humans belong to the same species doesn't mean they'll naturally get along. It's the same with our biological family, *Canidae*. In this group you'll find dogs, wolves, coyotes, dingos and jackals. We share certain similarities, but there's one thing every one of us has in common. We all hate foxes, the other *Canidae* member. In human family terms, they're like the really annoying brother-in-law. No one can pinpoint exactly why they're so irritating and insufferable; they just are.

Although foxes are related to us, they have vertical pupils, can climb trees, have retractable claws, pounce on their prey and are more active at night – so they actually have more in common with cats.

Maybe that's why we hate them.

FRIDGES

You know that big white thing that stands in the kitchen? It's not just another domestic appliance; it's a portal to a special, magical world.

Think of it as being similar to the wardrobe that can transport you to Narnia (I've always loved the works of C. S. Lewis – so chewable), but the world it leads to is somewhere far more important. The world that the fridge leads to is the world of food.

Seeing your owner open the door is an almost spiritual experience – it will be accompanied by a heavenly glow and canine angels yipping sweetly. Okay, I lied about the angels, but there *is* a bright light that casts its radiance over sausages, bacon, chicken, beef and a whole host of special treats.

The fridge will open many times during the day, usually so your owners can remove mundane items like milk, fizzy drinks or fruit juice. They see it as a chance to quench their thirst; you must see it as an opportunity to put on your best puppy-dog eyes and beg.

FRIDGE MAGNETS

What these are:
Ornamental magnets, sometimes adorned with the names of holiday destinations, which act as a permanent reminder of the depressing time you spent in boarding kennels waiting for your owners to return. Sometimes used simply for decoration; other times used as a means to attach their shopping lists, terrible children's drawings or photos of other humans.

What these are not:
Edible.

FRISBEE-CATCHING

Family-friendly movies and TV commercials for dog food have a lot to answer for. Sure, on screen, a dog leaping off the ground in slow motion to grasp a Frisbee in its mouth mid-flight is an act of grace, poise and lithe athleticism on a par with anything you'd see at the Bolshoi. But as you may have already discovered, the reality is remarkably different.

Balls are fine. They go up. They come down. And if they bounce, even the dimmest pit bull will have a pretty good idea of where they're going to land. Frisbees, however, have a mind of their own and can change trajectory even faster than we change our mind about where to pee. If you're in any doubt whatsoever about whether you have the necessary skills and eye/mouth co-ordination to catch a Frisbee, don't even try. Misjudge your leap and at best you'll miss the Frisbee completely and land ingloriously on your back. At worst you'll be hit in the mouth or head, causing you to lose not only self-esteem but possibly also consciousness.

CANINE COMMENT

Charley Sure, it starts out as a bit of harmless fun …

See also *Fetch*

GLOW-IN-THE-DARK EYES

Have you ever caught sight of yourself in the mirror and it looks like you've got glowing red or green eyes that make you resemble an evil hellhound rather than someone cuddly called Poochie? Fantastic, isn't it?

The truth is, you're not really possessed by some doggy

demon. This otherworldly glow is due to a special light-collecting membrane that makes our eyes look really creepy when viewed from a certain angle.

Having this membrane gives us two great advantages:

1. It helps us see better in the dark
2. We can freak out our owners

Isn't nature wonderful?

GOING OUT

You may hear your owner say that staying in is the new going out. They are lying.

For dogs, going out will never be replaced as our favourite leisure activity. Ever. Of course, by going out I don't mean shopping, catching a film, seeing an exhibition or eating at a fancy restaurant. I mean the back garden.

Being domesticated means we no longer have the free reign of woodland, forests or meadows, but even so, we still crave the fresh air and the feeling of something under our feet that isn't carpet or cheap wood-effect flooring.

Why do we like going out into the garden so much? Well, apart from an opportunity to explore our surroundings and chase birds or squirrels, it's a far more civilized place than the lounge or spare bedroom in which to defecate. However, the main reason we like to go out so often is because it really winds up our owners.

An insider's guide to going out

Step 1
Choose your moment; one where the need to go out causes the most disruption. Suggestions include the beginning of a new, highly regarded Nordic noir series, five minutes before the end of a critical sporting event, in the middle of a crucial phone call or when your owners have just fallen asleep.

Step 2
Position yourself between your owner and what they are currently doing. Stare intently at them with an exasperated expression.
If ignored, go to Step 3

Step 3
Whine or bark to be let out into the garden. Do this for as long as it takes your owner to get the message.

Step 4
Your owner will sigh, get up and reluctantly open the back door, usually remarking 'Not again!' or swearing. If it's at night, just before he opens the door he'll add, 'No barking!', fully understanding the absolute futility of this request.

Step 5
Go outside.

Step 6
Explore, chase, fetch, run, poop, pee or roll around in something unsuitable. Bark loudly.

Step 7

Whine or bark to be let back in again.

Step 8

Repeat steps 1 to 7 every ten to twenty minutes.

CANINE COMMENT

Molly Let me in. I want to go out again.

GRASS, EATING

You'll soon find out that one of the biggest differences between humans and us is how we each approach any given situation. As dogs we tend to act instinctively and just do things. People, on the other hand, really overthink. A great case in point is the matter of why, since we're predominantly carnivores, we love eating grass or other vegetation. Humans have pondered this issue for years and still don't really know the answer.

Why humans think we eat grass

- It's a natural remedy for upset stomachs: the grass

makes us vomit up anything disagreeable
- It gives us extra nutrients and fibre
- It compensates for a dietary deficiency
- It's a throwback to when we scavenged in the wild
- It's a sign of anxiety

Why we really eat grass
- We like the taste

GROOMING

If you hate bath time then you'll absolutely loathe going to the groomer's.

Sure, these places have cute names like Pawfection, Vanity Fur or Dapper Dogs, but that's just to conceal the fact that behind their attractive facades are some of the most terrifying places a dog can find itself.

Don't be deceived or get lulled into a false sense of security when you get there. There'll be a nice little reception area with water and a tempting bowl of treats and it will seem like you're checking into a swish boutique doggy hotel. However, the next thing you know your owner is handing you over to a complete stranger and you're taken into another room full of terrifying-looking equipment. It's like some sort of medieval torture chamber, but instead of racks, iron maidens and pliers you'll be exposed to clippers, de-matting combs and blaster-dryers. And they're the nicer examples.

You'll be muzzled, shackled to a table and then sheared, shaved, cropped, clipped, trimmed and brushed to within an inch of your life – and then placed in a cage to await collection.

And the person carrying all this out is likely to be far more suited to working at Guantanamo Bay than at a grooming salon – rinsing you will be undertaken with as much care and sensitivity as they'd no doubt apply to their jobs.

If Amnesty International ever knew the truth there'd be an outcry.

CANINE COMMENT

Polly A picture's worth a thousand words. Here are four: beware of the groomers.

HANDBAGS

If you're the sort of dog who can stand alongside a fully grown chihuahua or Pomeranian and still feel intimidated, then there's a good chance you'll find yourself being transported from place to place in one of these devices.

The advantage is that sometimes it's nice to be

carried about, particularly when you have little legs. The disadvantage is that you'll probably find yourself sharing the confined space with a Sophie Kinsella paperback, a grubby hairbrush, a packet of aspirin, assorted pens, a pocket mirror, tissues, bottles of perfume and/or water, tampons, a phone, a big tube of concealer and/or moisturizer, a half-used packet of chewing gum, headphones and sunglasses.

You may think the benefits outweigh the disadvantages, but think twice if you suffer from claustrophobia or have an acute fear of sitting on the sharp end of an eyebrow pencil.

CANINE COMMENT

Lulu My owner must be a magician. In moments she can change me from a dog to a fashion accessory.

HEAT, BEING ON

This is the stage in a female dog's reproductive cycle when she becomes receptive to mating with males. In human terms it's called 'being horny'.

If you've been spayed, you won't experience this change in your body, which happens twice a year and lasts for between two and three weeks. It's a time when your oestrogen levels will rise and you'll ovulate. You might also bleed and since there's currently no such invention as a doggy tampon, you have to be very careful not to stain your owner's carpet or furniture – just getting mud on the couch is cause for a bad enough scolding, but in this case … well, need I say more?

HOSEPIPES

These will be familiar to you if you live in a house with a garden. They look like vicious green snakes that spit water and, like a cobra, can be just as mesmerizing. Be on your guard: with a subtle flick of your owner's wrist they can go from being a method of watering plants to a device that delivers a spontaneous and unlooked-for bath.

HUMANS, OLD

These are humans that are about ten or more in our years. Having one of them as your owner can bring mixed blessings.

Advantage
- They tend to rely on us much more for companionship than their younger versions and because of this, really spoil us

Disadvantage
- We usually get blamed for their farts

HUMANS, YOUNG

These are the human equivalents of puppies, also known as children. There are a number of downsides when it comes to sharing a house with them, but one major benefit.

Disadvantages
- They pull our tails
- They bark back at us
- They hug us too tightly
- They pet us too hard

- They hide our toys
- They think it's funny to squirt us with water
- They stroke our fur THE WRONG WAY!
- They sit on our backs and yell, 'Horsey! Horsey!'

Advantages
- They have poor co-ordination and are more prone to dropping their food on the floor accidentally

INOCULATIONS

Canine parvovirus, canine distemper, leptospirosis, infectious canine hepatitis – I'm not sure what's worse, the sound of these diseases or their effects.

Fortunately for us, advances in medical science mean that our catching them can be prevented. Unfortunately for us, the way we're prevented from catching them is by a vet using a piece of equipment called a syringe. This syringe contains what humans refer to as a vaccine. This is good.

The syringe also contains a very pointy needle. This is very bad.

KENNEL

The human phrase 'in the dog house' means someone who's in disgrace.

This term should be applied to anyone who wants to make you sleep outside in some crappy wooden house that'll be covered in mould and infested with spiders before you can say, 'I'm bloody freezing!' From growling to howling, barking to begging, use any and all means at your disposal to resist attempts by your owners to make you sleep here. They will try and convince you that this alternative accommodation is warm and dry. Remember, living outdoors is neither.

CANINE COMMENT

Rex Me, sleep outside? In the garden? In a shack? You're having a laugh!

KENNEL NAMES

These are nothing to do with dog houses. Your kennel name is a sign of good breeding. Literally.

It's the human equivalent of being called Tarquin Ponsonby-Smythe, except it's even more ridiculous.

It is essentially your name (and sometimes your parents' names) added to your breeder's name. Except your breeder's name won't be something simple like George or Margaret; it'll be a completely unique one-word name registered with the Kennel Club, which at best will be unusual and at worst ludicrous or plain crazy.

A kennel name lets other dogs know you have a pedigree, but ask yourself, is it worth that status when you're called something like Oliver Abraxas Hazelnut Pennywhistle or Lovelace Hidalgo Cockspur Sweetsugardumpling?

CANINE COMMENT

Bertie I'm known in my area as Bertie. If any of my friends found out I am actually Engelbert Moon-Pilot Artemis Puffpuffbuttercup, my life wouldn't be worth living.

See also *Names*

KENNELS, BOARDING

Your owners will tell you these are doggy hotels – somewhere to stay while they're away on holiday. On the face of it, this sounds appealing: a chance for you to relax and be pampered in a different environment … it's like you're having your very own holiday!

The truth is somewhat different. Like human hotels, boarding kennels can straddle a similar quality divide. In my experience, however, most seem to be establishments that are run by people like Norman Bates rather than Conrad Hilton.

5 signs you're in really bad boarding kennels

1. There's a hair in your bed … and it's not yours.
2. There's a bitch on heat in the pen opposite you and a steady stream of visitors all night long.
3. You're kept awake at night by a dog whining, 'Help me! Help me!'
4. The operators have obviously confused the words 'boarding kennels' with the words 'detention camp'.
5. You come away with more fleas than you went in with.

KISSING

Humans think that when we lick them, it's the equivalent of a kiss. Fools!

They don't realize that it's just a throwback to our wild ancestry when we'd lick our mothers' faces as a signal that we were hungry and she should vomit up partially digested food.

As long as they continue to think it's a sign of affection rather than regurgitation, you'll continue to receive treats.

Don't stop them believing.

CANINE COMMENT

Murray Guess what part of me I was licking thirty seconds ago ...

LASERS

All it takes is a cheap laser pen and a flat surface and in next to no time you will be mesmerized by a dancing red or green dot, leaping from paw to paw and chasing it all round the room, up the wall and into any crannies you think it's hiding in.

Since their invention way back in the late 1950s, lasers have impacted many areas of human life – manufacturing, astronomy, entertainment, medicine, warfare, consumer electronics – and now, it seems, pet annoyance.

LEASHES: TANGLING FOR FUN AND ENJOYMENT

Humans say they put us on leashes to protect us from traffic and to make sure we don't run off and chase cats, squirrels or other dogs. This is true, to an extent, but the real reason is that they want to say to us, 'Hey, look at me. Who's the alpha male/female now, huh?'

It's the case, sadly, that when you're on a leash your owner usually has control … but that doesn't mean you can't have fun along the way. Just as, in a fight, Jackie Chan would use any object to his advantage, you can use the leash in the exact same way.

Method 1: The motion tangle

Suddenly criss-cross in front of or behind your owner without any warning. This will surprise them and result in a temporary loss of balance and an ungraceful recovery, revealing a comical lack of coordination. The effect will be far more dramatic if you're both running.

Method 2: The stationary tangle

When your owner stops in the street to talk to someone, adopt ninja mode and stealthily and silently walk around his legs a couple of times. If all goes according to plan he'll be so engrossed in conversation (more so if it involves any degree of flirtation) that as soon as he tries to walk off he'll lose two things: his balance and his pride.

CANINE COMMENT

Rollo Guess what happened next?

LEG-HUMPING: FAQS

Barking loudly at 4 a.m., peeing against your neighbour's new car or eating poop: if you're talking about embarrassing behaviour, these actions pale into insignificance when it comes to leg-humping. It's the one thing guaranteed to turn your owner's face redder than a red setter, particularly when it involves guests.

Why do I want to do it?
  A. To cause maximum embarrassment to your owner
  B. It feels good
Your reasons for leg-humping should be a combination of A and B. Most humans think we leg-hump because it's an outlet for our sexual urges. Well, a lot of the time it is, but at other times it's because we're showing dominance or are just being playful.

It's good that humans think we're being overly sexual, as this causes them the most discomfort. Exploit this fact.

Is it natural for a dog to hump a human's leg?
Yes. But remember, under no circumstances is it natural if the roles are reversed.

Does humping a human's leg mean I'm attracted to them?
Not at all. You're just scratching a biological itch. The leg might belong to someone who looks like a Hollywood A-lister or someone you're more likely to see on a daytime chat show. To us it doesn't matter – it's just something nice to rub against.

Thank god for that. My owner bears more than a passing resemblance to a hair-lipped bulldog chewing a stinging nettle, and I was afraid I'd lost any semblance of self-esteem.
You've got nothing to worry about.

I also have an urge to hump furniture.
Hmm. Ugly owner or table leg ... it's a no-brainer.

MAILMEN

These uniformed intruders are persistent. They approach your house on an almost daily basis. You bark; they turn around, walk back up the drive and leave.

But the next day, they're back.

And the day after that.

And the day after that.

Won't they ever learn that they're not wanted?

You always have to be on your guard against mailmen. Not only do they try their luck encroaching on our territory, but they are also harbingers of doom. You know that letter your owner got telling him that you had to visit the vet for your booster shot? The mailman was involved.

MANGE

It's a close-run thing as to which sounds worse: mange, or the actual name for this very embarrassing skin disease, canine scabies.

If you suffer from mange you should hope for two things:
1. Your owners get you treated as soon as possible.
2. They have the sense and decency to pronounce it like the second syllable in the dessert 'blancmange'. This gives the condition a more sophisticated, European feel and reduces the stigma (if not the itching).

MARKING YOUR TERRITORY

As dogs we have it easy when it comes to staking a claim as to what constitutes our territory. Piss-easy, in fact.

All you have to do is urinate on the area you want to designate as your space and the signature scent of your pee means other dogs know it's yours. That bit of the garden from the paving to the large rose bush? Just cock your leg. That area from the end of the driveway to the corner? Just cock your leg.

That's all you need to do to indicate your land. No spending money, no lengthy form-filling, no dealing with bureaucratic local authorities or greedy lawyers. There are only two limiting factors to how much territory you can have. The first is your imagination and the second is the capacity of your bladder.

FURNITURE AS TERRITORY

Your territory doesn't have to be space outside your house. It can be your favourite chair, the couch or your owner's bed, which you lie on when no one's home. In this case it's not advisable to urinate on it to mark your space. Instead, rubbing your coat and face against the fabric will transfer your natural scent. Your owners will appreciate this method far more.

CANINE COMMENT

Milo Thanks to my unnaturally large bladder, I can lay claim to this entire field.

See also *Territory*

MATING

If you're inexperienced in the ways of love, I have two words of advice: don't worry. When the time comes, as a dog, you'll find the process comes naturally and, compared to the way humans do it, it's simplicity itself.

A typical human mating ritual involves

- Copious amounts of alcohol
- Mixed messages
- Frustration
- Confusion
- Disappointment
- Embarrassment
- Repercussions
- Regrets

A typical dog mating ritual involves

- The female presenting her hindquarters
- Er … that's it

Special advice

If you sleep in your owner's bedroom, you may be woken up by them mating. When this happens, get out of your bed or basket and stare at them. This will make them feel very awkward and will usually curtail the process. In this instance, your status changes from pet to contraceptive.

MICROCHIPS

Most of you will have had these implanted under your skin when you were a puppy. And by implanted I mean you'll have had a large needle inserted under the skin between your shoulder blades. Once fitted, you can simply forget it. The benefit is that if you're ever found wandering, an animal shelter or vet can scan you and reunite you with your owner. The downside is that it's impossible to be the canine equivalent of Jason Bourne and go off the grid. You win some, you lose some.

MIXED BREEDS

If you are one, then be proud of your heritage and be thankful that society's attitudes are changing. Way back when, mixed-breeds would be taunted with the insult 'mongrel'. Thankfully that name is slowly being replaced with the term 'love child'.

CANINE COMMENT

Coco Mongrel? As a cockapoo, please refer to me as a Designer Crossbreed.

MUZZLES

A muzzle says more about you than words ever can. Unfortunately, it usually says, 'I'm the doggy version of Hannibal Lecter.' And it's difficult to put a positive spin on that, whichever way you look at it.

Although they prevent you from biting, most muzzles do allow you to drink and eat. Even if that food is liver and some fava beans …

CANINE COMMENT

Bullet Don't judge a book by its cover … although the reason I'm wearing this is to prevent me eating books.

NAMES

As the saying goes, 'You can choose where you pee, but you can't choose your name.' Humans insist on giving us monikers that fall into one of four categories: appropriate, overly aggressive, overly noble, or just plain odd. Of course, that's fine if you like your name or if it accurately sums up your character, appearance or temperament, like Smiler, Blackie or Diablo.

The problem comes when we're given a name that humans think is really funny or cute and it's plainly not.

So what can a dog do? Unfortunately, not a lot. Like us, a name is for life.

Sure, you can point-blank refuse to respond to that name, but that's only likely to exasperate your owner and probably get you enrolled in an obedience class (and that should be avoided at all costs). The only alternative is to learn to accept it, as irritating or humiliating as it might be.

After all, if humans choose to call their offspring India, Daisy Boo, Apple or Harper Seven then is it any wonder that they'd choose to call their new Shih Tzu puppy Colin?

Examples of the four types of dog names bestowed by humans

Appropriate	Overly aggressive	Overly noble	Just plain odd
Cody, Rex, Prince, Missy, Bailey, Marley, Gizmo, Coco, Milo, Spot, Molly, Rover, Bella, Charley	Killer, Razor, Steel, Boss, Nitro, Bullet, Diablo, Judas, Ripper, Blade, Magnum, Terminator	Maxwell Woofington, Lord Dogstone-Petsworthy, Sir Barky of Boneington End, Lady Alice von Furrycoat	Nigel, Dave, Clifford

CANINE COMMENT

Keith I absolutely hate my name. Keith should be a carpet fitter or a plumber, not a Cavalier King Charles spaniel.

Courtney Really? REALLY? Do I look like a bloody Courtney?!

NEEDY OWNERS

Having a needy owner is fine, up to a degree. You'll get lots of affection, toys and treats but also run the risk of being smothered by their love … sometimes literally, by an overabundance of hugs. Dogs need their own space too, so it might be time to make yourself scarce the moment you hear one of the following phrases.

Things owners say that indicate they're needy

- You're the only one that understands me
- Who needs a boyfriend when I have you?
- What would I do without you?
- You're the first, the last, my everything
- Every breath in your lungs is a tiny, beautiful gift to me

Things owners say that indicate they're extremely needy

- I wish I could marry you

NEUTERING

This section is for male dogs. Females should see *Spaying.*

Our owners will naturally be concerned about you fathering lots of unwanted puppies, but instead of taking the time to lecture us on abstinence or making us wear a purity ring, they remove our testicles.

Yes. Both of them.

Humans are convinced this is the right thing to do by telling themselves that it will also prevent cancer and prostate problems. They call the procedure neutering, as it makes them feel less guilty than calling it 'castration'.

I won't go into detail here about what the whole neutering process entails, except to say it involves something sharp and pointy in the vicinity of your genital area. If I tell you any more you'll run away from home.

3 other aspects of neutering that are even more troubling

If having someone interfere with your undercarriage without you signing a consent form isn't upsetting enough, then the following will make you more distraught.

1. Because the operation involves a general anaesthetic, you won't be able to eat for several hours beforehand. SEVERAL HOURS!
2. You'll have your undercarriage shaved. Going to

the park afterwards without your testicles can really damage your self-esteem. Sporting a reverse-Brazilian just compounds the problem.

3. To stop you licking the wound you'll probably have to wear the Cone of Shame. This is often more distressing than the whole neutering procedure.

What to do after the operation

1. Have plenty of rest.
2. Practise an expression that combines these four emotions simultaneously: resignation, bitterness, anger and resentment.
3. Maintain that look until your owners become immune to its effects and realize you recovered from your trauma ages ago and are now simply faking it.

CANINE COMMENT

Rocky Before I was neutered I used to chase cats, mount other dogs and bark loudly at the mailman. Now I spend my time staring at the live feed of *Big Brother* or looking wistfully out of the window.

PACKS, MAINTAINING YOUR POSITION IN

Back when we were wolves rather than dogs, we ran around in packs, hunting for food and defending our territory. It was exciting and dangerous. It was like being in a tough street gang but without the need to wear bandanas.

Nowadays the only time we get to run around in a pack is in the park, where our relationships with other dogs are brief and casual – similar to what humans experience from internet dating.

Our change in circumstances from eking out an existence in the wild to curling up in an armchair in the suburbs has meant the nature of our pack has also changed: it's now our owners and their family. Despite this new dynamic, it's just as important for us to exert dominance in our present-day pack.

What to do in order to ensure your position as the alpha male/female within your pack

Then	Now
Have an aggressive and forceful personality	Lie in the hall or in doorways so people have to step around you
Fight tooth and claw to protect your territory	Pull hard on the leash
Lead the hunt	Refuse to fetch the stick

Be the first to bring down the prey	Jump on the couch the moment your owner wants to watch television and when asked to move, wriggle yourself into an even more comfortable position
Attack any challengers to your authority	Nudge and stare a lot

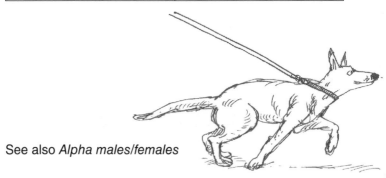

See also *Alpha males/females*

POINTING

On many occasions your owner will make a fist and extend his forefinger.* At the same time he'll exclaim the word, 'Look!' and expect you to move your head excitedly in the direction of his finger.

There should really be only one reaction to this command: **stare straight at his finger; never at where he is pointing.**

This is incredibly frustrating for your owner, who'll insist on repeating 'Look!' over and over again. There will be an obvious correlation between his exasperation and the volume of his command, but ignore this. The more he says 'Look!', the more you should stare at his finger.

Don't worry, you won't be missing out on anything. It is incredibly unlikely that he will be pointing to anything actually worth looking at, like the unopened door to a pet food factory or a bunch of cats on a day out. It will inevitably be something boring, like a stick.

*The one next to the thumb that is fun to nip.

POOPING: FAQS

My owner insists on looking at me when I take a dump. What can I do?

No creature likes someone looking at them while they defecate. Not only is it off-putting, it's also very creepy. If they insist, all you can do is give them your best, 'Hey, can I have a little privacy?' look and carry on.

Should I always poop in the same place on my walk?

Are you crazy? Of course not. It's fun to keep your owner guessing.

When is the best time to want to poop?

Whenever it will cause maximum inconvenience. Suggestions include:

- Two minutes after you've just pooped
- In the middle of crossing a very busy road
- Any time (and anywhere) you shouldn't

How many times should I poop while I'm on a walk?
One more than the number of poop bags your owner is carrying.

Is it appropriate to do a 'booty scoot' to clean my butt?
Of course. Think of a grass verge or the side of the road as nature's toilet paper.

It usually takes me ages to find the perfect place to poop. I find somewhere, sniff, turn around in circles, move on a few feet, sniff again, turn some more, move back to the original spot, sniff again, move on a few more feet, sniff again, turn around a bit more, move another few feet, do some more turning, then sniff again until eventually I find the right place, which is usually the original spot. This whole process really, really exasperates my owner.
And your point is?

CANINE COMMENT

Spot Hey! A little privacy please!

PUDDLES, MUDDY

These exist for two reasons and two reasons only:

1. For you to roll in.
2. For you to drink from.

PUPPY-DOG EYES

When it comes to influencing and manipulating your owners, the most important weapon in your armoury is the ability to look pathetic.

Often employed when begging is fruitless, puppy-dog eyes are most frequently put to good use to shame your owners into taking you for a walk or to make them feel guilty about going out and leaving you alone.

How to make puppy-dog eyes

As I said in the section on Begging (see page 20), you don't have to be a puppy in order to have puppy-dog eyes. It's not just a question of the eyes, though; there are some subtle head movements that can maximize the feelings of guilt you want to evoke in your owners.

- Tilt your head down
- Think of something really sad
- Raise your eyes so you're looking through your lashes
- Hunch your shoulders
- Keep shifting your weight from one front paw to the other

To make your owner feel extra shame
- Angle your head slightly to one side. This is a small move, but one that will have a disproportionately significant effect

To make your owners feel as guilty as hell
- Do all of the above with your head resting on your owner's knee or lap

HOW TO LOOK REALLY, REALLY SAD

The key to successfully pulling off puppy-dog eyes is, obviously, the ability to look really sad. Of course, this could be because you're genuinely sad at the thought of being left alone for four hours (unlikely), but in order to play the required part and increase your owner's guilt, the impression you have to give is that of someone much, much sadder. These are some of the things you can imagine to achieve the desired effect:

- The park is closed
- All the lamp posts in the street have been removed
- You chased and caught a bouncing ball and felt absolutely no sense of achievement
- Cats universally extend the paw of friendship towards dogs

CANINE COMMENT

Bella By practising in front of a mirror four times a day I can now cause instant guilt in my owner with a mere glance.

See also *Begging*

RABIES

There are only three things you really need to know about rabies, or as many dogs say in hushed tones, 'the R word':

1. It's a virus that affects your brain and central nervous system.
2. It's usually fatal.
3. You really don't want to catch it.

And just to make it even worse, there are actually two forms of rabies. One is called furious rabies and causes increased aggression. The other is called paralytic rabies and it causes … well, the clue's in the name, duh!

Although rabies has been virtually eradicated in the UK, many myths about it still persist. Things like, 'You can catch it from sharing another dog's bowl' or 'I'm a pit bull so I can't catch it', so I thought I'd better set the record straight.

Correcting some common misconceptions about rabies

- Being bitten does not mean you'll contract rabies: you can only catch it by being bitten by a mammal carrying the virus. Being playfully nipped by a Chihuahua or dachshund in the park should just be seen as annoying or embarrassing rather than an automatic death sentence
- Excessive excitability is not an automatic sign that you have rabies. It could be because your owners are frying sausages
- Likewise, foaming at the mouth might not signify infection. It might be because you've exercised a little too much, have an upset stomach or have just chewed a tube of toothpaste

- Anyone can be susceptible to rabies, irrespective of their breeding. Just because you're called Binky Toureg Frilly-Chum Tatiana-Winthrop and have been a Crufts Champion of Champions doesn't make you immune
- Cats can transmit rabies; so can kittens. Cute doesn't mean harmless
- Biting someone without warning doesn't necessarily mean you've developed rabies. It could just mean you're very naughty

IMPORTANT ADVICE

If you *are* bitten by a creature with rabies and your owner is aware, don't resist being taken to the vet. Honestly, this is not the time to take a stance.

SELECTIVE HEARING

Our hearing is vastly superior to that of humans. We can hear over much greater distances, we can hear frequencies they can only dream of and some of us can even swivel our ears in the direction of the sound. Wicked!

All these abilities come in useful in everyday life, but by far the best advantage of our hearing is **our capacity to filter out unwanted sounds**. And by unwanted sounds I don't only mean our ability not to hear owners shouting 'Fetch!' from a distance of ten feet, or managing to hear them opening a packet of crisps two streets away, I'm talking about filtering out unwanted parts of conversation. This happens automatically – sometimes almost as a reflex.

What your owner says	What you hear
I'll take you for a walk after I've had a nap	I'll take you for a walk
It's dinner time when I say it's dinner time!	It's dinner time!
I'm not just giving you a treat. You have to earn it!	Treat!
It's late. You can only go outside if you don't bark!	Bark!

SEPARATION ANXIETY

Owners have a habit of disappearing, and while this can be disconcerting at times, it's a natural part of the dog–owner relationship. The amount of time they're gone can vary from a few minutes (they're most likely sitting on the toilet) to a few weeks (they're most likely sitting on a sun-lounger).

Even being alone for just two or three hours can lead to what's known as separation anxiety – the fear that your owner won't return – and the realization that this would therefore jeopardize your future supply of food, walkies, petting and treats.

Separation anxiety can manifest itself in a number of ways: peeing, pooping, howling, barking, pacing, chewing, digging or other destructive behaviour. Sometimes it's a combination of these, and when you add in something like eating your own poop, it's never a pretty sight.

There's no easy solution to separation anxiety, but the following might put your mind at rest and make you a little less apprehensive.

5 things to remember that help reduce separation anxiety

- He might be gone a while (like if he's taken his phone into the bathroom to play Candy Crush) but your owner *will* make a reappearance
- The bathroom door is not a portal to another dimension

123

- There is a proportional relationship between the length of time your owner is away and the quality of treat he usually returns with
- The metal thing your owner gets into just before he disappears is only a Ford Focus. He is not being kidnapped by an evil Decepticon
- Your owner is likely to be suffering from separation anxiety too

CANINE COMMENT

Ralph 'I'll only be a minute,' she said. If I had a treat for every time I'd heard that!

SHOES

Loafers, sneakers, slingbacks, boots, stilettos, slippers, flip-flops, moccasins and sandals. An almost endless variety of textures and tastes … and all with a deliciously footy flavour. Chewing slowly on a well-worn leather brogue is like you've died and gone to doggy heaven. The problem, however, stems from humans' illogical attachment to shoes. Since we don't wear them it's difficult to appreciate why they get so annoyed when we destroy their footwear. That's why, if you're going to chew a shoe, you must make sure you hide the evidence afterwards. Along with the other one of the pair.

CANINE COMMENT

Boomer With a little practice it doesn't take long to appreciate the subtle difference in taste between a Christian Louboutin and a Manolo Blahnik.

See also *Chewing*

SLEEPING

One of the best things about being a dog is how much we get to sleep each day. It's brilliant! If your owner were inactive for that length of time it would be a sign that they were either a student or worked for local government, but when we do it, no one gives a second thought.

It's difficult to estimate accurately how long you should sleep each day. The average is twelve to fourteen hours, but there are so many factors involved – your age, your breed, your health, your diet and your environment. The only thing you need to know is that in terms of hours, it's 'a lot'.

But why do we sleep so long? No one knows, and anyway, who cares? Just make the most of it.

If you can't be bothered to go out for a walk or play with that stupid toy, simply **pretend to be asleep**. Find a nice warm spot, curl up, close your eyes and twitch and flick your paws from time to time to indicate you're dreaming about chasing bunnies or similar.

Your owners will have absolutely no idea you're faking it.

CANINE COMMENT

Sidney Twelve to fourteen hours sleep a day? Sure. More if I lie in.

SMELLING THINGS

From lamp posts to lilies and food bins to fox poop, smelling things is usually the highlight of our walks – if not our entire day.

If there were a decaying skunk carcass at the side of the road, we'd sniff it. If raw sewage were spewing from a burst pipe, we'd smell that. If a truck carrying Britney Spears' signature perfume had crashed and slewed its entire contents across the street, we'd even smell that.

Our sensitive noses can detect pheromones of humans and other animals, but more importantly, it gives us an opportunity to aggravate our owners. It's not enough to stop and sniff every object you pass; you have to smell each one ever so slowly, methodically and most vitally of all, repeatedly. Each aroma and bouquet has to be savoured. Take in that essence and let it flow leisurely over your scent receptors. Make your first impression. Sniff some more and find the heart of the smell. Sniff more and appreciate its body, its character and its blend.

Savour those smells

Only by taking your time can you truly appreciate the myriad subtle fragrances in every smell. Here's a description of a few key odours:

- That apple tree: fruity with an intoxicating old-fashioned musk and notes of urine
- That bench: a subtle cedar with a balm of rust and notes of urine
- That fence: a redolence of creosote with a whisper of pine and notes of urine

See also *Butt-sniffing, Crotch-sniffing*

SPAYING

This section is for females. Male dogs should see *Neutering* on page 111 (well, only if you don't mind being disturbed and upset).

Spaying is the female version of neutering and, if I can offer any consolation if you're to undergo this procedure, it's that it's simpler to forget you had ovaries and a uterus than testicles, believe me.

The upside of the operation is that you won't get pregnant or get unwanted attention from male dogs when you're in heat – and that's got to be worth having surgery for. It also reduces the likelihood of having breast cancer and, although dogs don't get involved with fun runs and wearing pink tutus, it is a condition that female dogs can suffer from. The downside of being spayed is that you can't go outside for about ten days after the operation. It's not the soreness that hurts; it's being subjected to ten days of daytime television that causes the most distress.

CANINE COMMENT

Missy To be honest, I would have preferred a lecture on abstinence.

SQUIRRELS

There are two things you need to know about squirrels:
1. No matter how hard we try and fight the feeling, we instinctively want to chase and catch them.
2. No matter how hard we try, we never can.

There's something about seeing that bushy tail that makes us see a red mist. We ignore what we're doing, stop listening to our owners and disregard all thoughts of our own safety. Losing control like this is distressing, but what's more worrying is that despite the knowledge that they're rodents and no matter how cute you are, people will always find a squirrel sitting up on its back legs holding an acorn in its little paws cuter.

Sometimes even cuter than kittens.

STARING

Like glow-in-the-dark eyes (see page 85), staring is a great way to have fun with your owner. The key to a successful stare is not, as you may think, simply gazing intently at your owner with your eyes wide open. While that can be quite unsettling, it's possible to use the stare for far more dramatic effect.

The following actions will turn disconcerting staring into 'freak-them-out' staring.

Method 1: Look past your owner at some imaginary object just over their shoulder.
Method 2: Run into the hall and suddenly stare at the front door (for enhanced effect, start barking).

In both cases you must give the impression that you can definitely see something they can't. Something like a Victorian child.

STICKS

Beware the stick. Your owner might insist on throwing one for you to fetch, but these seemingly innocent bits of trees are fraught with issues.

WHY STICKS ARE NO FUN

- You can get splinters embedded in your gums or tongue
- A piece might break off and block your digestive tract or puncture a lung
- They don't bounce

CANINE COMMENT

Baxter Sticks? Yeah ... not that exciting.

SUN, LYING IN THE

Just because we can't get suntans doesn't mean we don't love the sun. That's why, given half a chance, you'll find us warming ourselves in the hallway, by the open back door or on a patio.

However, the thing we like almost as much as the sun is the shade.

This is a typical way to spend a morning in the summer months:

Step 1: Lie in sun
Step 2: Get too hot
Step 3: Find shade
Step 4: Get too cold
Step 5: Repeat Steps 1 to 4 until dinner time

SWIMMING

Some dogs take to water like ducks. If you're a Portuguese water dog or an Irish water spaniel, you'll know what I mean. You're the Michael Phelps of the doggy world: confident, fast and floaty.

Breeds that are heavyset with big heads or short stubby legs (bulldogs, pugs and basset hounds, I'm talking to you) look like a drowning accident waiting to happen.

What to do when you're in water

From puddles to pools, streams to the sea, water can take many forms. To determine an appropriate course of action when you're in water, ask yourself, 'Can I touch the bottom?' If the answer is 'yes', then you can walk or run around, splashing as much as you like with no fear for your own safety. If the answer is 'no', then unless you start swimming you will sink to the bottom. If there's just one piece of advice you remember from this entire book, let it be this: dogs can't breathe water.

How to swim
If you're a breed that *can* swim (see previous page), then follow these simple actions:
A. Keep your head above the surface
B. Make a running motion

That's it! What you're doing is called, appropriately enough, the 'doggy paddle', and while it isn't the most gracious of swimming strokes, it's enough to propel you around and keep you afloat.

Buoyancy aids
Your owner might not have faith in your swimming ability and may make you wear a doggy life jacket. These are brightly coloured and have a handle on the back so you can be carried around like a furry briefcase.

Advantages: They'll help keep you afloat and might save your life.

Disadvantages: Other dogs will laugh at you.

SPECIAL ADVICE FOR SWIMMING IN THE SEA, A LAKE OR A RIVER

A. Before it's time to go home, make sure you go for a walk along the shore or bank
B. Look for any dead fish that might have been deposited there
C. Roll around on them

CANINE COMMENT

Madison That's what they think ...

See also *Drying off*

TAILS

Humans suffer from the misconception that a wagging tail always means a happy dog. Sometimes it does; other times it doesn't. It all depends on how high you're holding your tail, which direction it's wagging, how fast it's wagging, and even if the wag also involves your hips. And if that's not confusing enough, the signals differ according to your breed anyway – some of us will carry our tail upright and curled when we're relaxed. Others will carry it low. And some dogs will wag their tail to show they're scared or insecure, or even as a warning.

Dogs, of course, completely understand these subtleties, but humans have absolutely no idea what you're trying to communicate with your tail – that's why it's best to rely on verbal communication with people.

Remember, a bark is worth a thousand wags.

The 4 reasons humans think we have tails

1. To communicate various emotions
2. To provide balance when running and turning
3. To provide stability when swimming
4. To fan our pheromones

The 4 reasons we really have tails

1. It's something to chase when we get bored
2. To knock things over
3. To thump against our owner's bedroom door at six in the morning to wake him or her up
4. To obstruct any vet trying to insert a rectal thermometer

TELEVISION

If you find the whole concept of television and the mechanics and process of transmitting sound and images confusing, don't worry. All you need to know about TV is that it exists for two purposes:

1. To entertain humans.
2. To make them feel less guilty when they leave us alone in the house for long periods of time.

With regards to 2, what humans fail to appreciate is that despite them fussing over which station to leave it on and adjusting the volume for us, we have ABSOLUTELY NO INTEREST in watching TV when they're out.

The reason? It's not because we have very limited colour vision or our brains process images at a different frame rate –

it's just that there's one thing even more unbelievably tedious than waiting for our owners' return: daytime television.

CANINE COMMENT

Buster Reruns of *Neighbours* and shows about gardening or home improvement. You call it light entertainment? I call it animal cruelty.

Pixie I like this chew toy.

TERRITORY

Some dogs call it their territory. To others it's their domain, their patch, their turf or their manor. The name isn't important, but what it represents is. Whether it's used for sleeping, running, playing, digging, chasing, sniffing or playing with a ball, your territory is the area you consider to be yours and yours alone. Well, I say yours alone, but the hard fact is that you usually have to share it with your owners and their immediate family. It's a thing that goes back thousands and thousands of years, when we shared caves with early man. They gave us shelter and warmth and we helped them hunt. Meh. What can you do about it?

Anyway, the whole concept of territory isn't really complicated. And there are just two things you are supposed to do with it:

1. Make sure others know about it.
2. Defend it from intruders.

Just remember, it's your dog-given right to have your own space. Don't let any other creature take it away from you.

Intruders

These come in many guises. In the house it usually means strangers and strange animals (like your owner's friend's yappy Pomeranian), while in the garden it might also include birds, pesky neighbourhood cats and squirrels. It doesn't actually matter who the interlopers are, your duty is to protect your territory at all costs.

If you ignore this instinct then as soon as your back is turned the trespasser could have stolen not only your food, your water, your bone or your favourite squeaky chew toy, but he could also be sitting on your favourite chair (a crime so heinous it really doesn't bear thinking about).

2 things to remember about territory

1. Territory isn't just limited to the space your owners have a mortgage on. In the dog world it can also extend to the driveway, the garage, your road and even the surrounding streets.
2. The more territory you have, the harder it is to defend. Remember that when you decide to mark your turf as the entire park.

See also *Marking your territory*

THUNDERSTORMS

Thunder can make the most dominant alpha male behave like a scaredy-cat, but however you react, just remember it's completely natural for dogs to exhibit some level of uneasiness. This can manifest itself in different ways. Some dogs experience a feeling of mild anxiety, while for others the effect is blind panic and absolute dread terror.

For most of us, it's the fear of the unknown that causes distress, so the first thing to do is to establish what thunder is and isn't.

WHAT THUNDER IS

A sonic shock wave caused by a lightning bolt.

WHAT THUNDER ISN'T

The sound of the angry dog gods barking in doggy heaven.

Understanding that thunder is a completely natural weather phenomenon and that it won't harm you enables you to think clearly when thunder does occur. And by thinking clearly, I mean thinking about thunder as a means to do all the things you're not usually allowed to do in the house. This includes barking at the top of your voice, going into rooms you're not allowed to, chewing shoes and, of course, peeing or pooping in them.

Your owner will attribute any unusual bad behaviour to you being upset by the loud noise. Not only will you be forgiven, there's a good chance you'll probably be hugged and given a treat.

Stormy weather – now that's definitely something worth praying to the dog gods for.

CANINE COMMENT

Gizmo Okay, it might be a natural phenomenon, but just let me know when it's over.

See also *Fireworks*

TO-DO LIST

Even the most organized dogs can feel overwhelmed by the amount of things they have to do every day. Sometimes you might forget to do something important like begging for human food; other times you might worry about whether you should be licking, scratching or rubbing ... and then run out of time to do one of them.

Don't fret! All you need is a Doggy To-Do List. It's simply a prioritized list of all the tasks that you need to carry out so that you don't forget anything important. By prioritizing tasks, you'll know what needs your immediate attention and what you can leave for later.

Below is a typical one, but you'll have to devise your own according to your routine and your needs

DOGGY TO-DO LIST

[ ] Wake up
[ ] Sleep
[ ] Forwards stretch
[ ] Yawn
[ ] Backwards stretch
[ ] Drink
[ ] Scratch left ear
[ ] Scratch right ear
[ ] Poop/Pee
[ ] Lick genitals
[ ] Full body shake
[ ] Eat
[ ] Drink
[ ] Chew something
[ ] Bark at mailman
[ ] Nap
[ ] Rub self against couch
[ ] Sleep
[ ] Walkies
[ ] Chase something
[ ] Poop/Pee
[ ] Play fetch
[ ] Scratch left ear
[ ] Scratch right ear

[ ] Drink
[ ] Nap
[ ] Lick genitals
[ ] Full body shake
[ ] Chew something
[ ] Walkies
[ ] Forwards stretch
[ ] Poop/Pee
[ ] Rub self against
    armchair
[ ] Nap
[ ] Backwards stretch
[ ] Eat
[ ] Drink
[ ] Beg for human food
[ ] Nap
[ ] Lick genitals
[ ] Poop/Pee
[ ] Nap
[ ] Scratch left ear
[ ] Scratch right ear
[ ] Drink
[ ] Sleep

Zoey Before I had a Doggy To-Do List I used to get in a real state! Now I know when to nap and when to poop. It's changed my life.

TOILET PAPER

Not having opposable thumbs makes it difficult for dogs to express their creativity. We can't hold a paintbrush or a pen, sculpt or play most musical instruments, for example, but what we can do is drag a toilet roll all around the house.

Your owner will view this with a combination of amusement and annoyance, yet they fail to appreciate the many subtle ways the toilet paper can be strewn. For example, there's neo-minimalism, where you leave four or five pieces of toilet paper on the floor in what appear to be random geometric forms, or abstract expressionism, where you pull off paper and run through the house changing direction spontaneously.

Don't let your owner's complaints stifle your creativity. Remember that inside every dog is a canine Kandinsky waiting to get out.

CANINE COMMENT

Cody I express myself through my toilet paper art. I call this particular technique Shredism.

See also *Toilets*

TOILETS

Also known by a whole host of other names like loo, john, WC, lavatory or bog, the toilet is that big white thing made of porcelain in the bathroom or, in some cases, a small separate room. You may have walked past when the door was ajar and seen your owner sitting on it and wondered what he was doing.

Well, this is where humans play on their phones and read; it's also a place where they pee and poop. Think of it as a sort of high-tech litter tray. However, it serves another more important purpose for you: a perpetual supply of cool, clean drinking water.

Worried about cleanliness? Don't be. You know that swooshing noise you hear from outside? That's the toilet cleaning itself. Plus, if you've ever drunk from puddles (and

I know you have) then it's obvious that hygiene isn't one of your top priorities.

N.B. If your owner is on the toilet and the door is ajar, go in and stare at them. See how they like it.

CANINE COMMENT

Rosie To be honest, you're better off using the garden or the street. It's far less complicated.

TRAINING: FAQS

In your early years there will probably come a time when your owner decides that you need training. This is a process that usually lasts for six to eight weeks, during which time you'll be expected to learn a number of so-called 'obedience commands'. A lot of dogs worry about what this entails, so I've compiled the following questions and answers to put your minds at rest.

How will I know I'm being trained?
There are three sure-fire signs:

1. You'll find yourself standing in a circle next to other dogs and their owners in a cold community hall, or an even colder park or field.

2. You're being shouted at by an overzealous ex-police dog handler or a self-righteous spinster.
3. You're soooooo bored.

Six to eight weeks? That's a long time learning stuff. Will I have to complete all the lessons?

It's highly unlikely. Your owner will get fed up before you do.

Are these obedience commands difficult to learn?

Difficult? How hard is it to learn how to sit or lie down? To think we'd actually struggle to understand these directives, our owners must take us for morons. Or cats.

So it's good to show our owners as soon as possible that we understand these commands?

No! You're nearly at the end of this book; haven't you learned anything I've taught you yet? By all means, make sure you know the commands, but under no circumstances should you let your owners know that you do.

But won't they think we're dumb?

Yes, that's exactly what we want them to think. Your owners will attribute the reason you ignore the commands to the fact you're a less intelligent life form. They'll have absolutely no idea we're wantonly disobeying them.

So what you're saying is that by pretending not to understand the commands we can do whatever we damn well want?

Precisely! We can sit when our owner shouts 'heel'; we can stay when she shouts 'come'. We don't even have to drop it when she says 'drop it'. Your owner will be infuriated and frustrated by your non-compliance. Result!

CANINE COMMENT

Duke Of course I know the command to sit ...

VACUUM CLEANERS

You know that dark cave in your house? Well, the truth is it's not really a dark cave: it's the cupboard under the stairs. And you know the dragon that lives there isn't really a dragon? It's a vacuum cleaner.

This is a machine humans use to clean the house, a process that includes picking up your shed hair. And while vacuum cleaners don't breathe fire like dragons, they do emit a loud roar and can be just as terrifying. The good thing, though, is that the scary noise doesn't last for long.

You'll probably hear it about twice a week (more frequently if you moult a lot), although if you live with just a male human, you'll only hear this noise on rare occasions.

VEGETABLES

I know it's hard to believe, but there is one foodstuff even more bland and unexciting than dry dog food. Humans call it the vegetable. Vegetables come in many shapes and colours (well, that's not strictly true, as most of the colours tend to be shades of green). However, apart from the carrot, which is crunchy like a dental chew stick, all the other vegetables are unbelievably tasteless and mind-numbingly dull.

Sometimes, with a completely misjudged sense that they should improve our nutrition, your owners might decide to supplement your normal diet with vegetables, but be on your guard: some are really poisonous to us. Onions, garlic, chives, mushrooms, rhubarb, green tomatoes, raw potatoes and avocado are all toxic to dogs.

When it comes to your health, don't take any chances. Avoid all vegetables.

CANINE COMMENT

Goldie Five a day? How about none a day?

VETS

Put simply, vets are animal doctors – the people who'll remove not only a thorn from your paw, but also your testicles.

Sure, they have fancy initials after their names, but all these do is disguise the fact that they weren't clever enough to train to become human doctors. As such, vets clearly take their resentment out on us – and other animals. Each time you're on their examination table, they think, 'I could have been a world-leading neurosurgeon. Instead I'm examining this schnauzer for mange.' These frustrations usually take the form of rough handling and a degree of prodding and poking usually associated with someone sorting fruit rather than anything connected with the medical profession.

5 reasons why we hate vets

- They shame us by telling us we have worms
- And that we're overweight
- They're the ones who recommend the Cone of Shame

- Three words: anal gland draining
- One word: vaccinations

A guide to what to expect at the vet

Waiting room
An opportunity to bark or be barked at. On the plus side, though, there are usually lots of cats in carriers that you can intimidate without fear of being scratched or hissed at.

Reception desk
Gives the impression you're at a swish hotel that prides itself on providing outstanding comfort for its customers. Nothing could be further from the truth.

The scales
These exist just so the vet can sell your owner expensive diet dog food.

The examination table
Stainless steel surface that offers two things: a cold surface for your bottom and a potentially painful drop on to a hard floor.

X-ray room
If you've swallowed something you shouldn't, this is the place to find out. Socks, keys, screws, rocks, small toys, bones, Lego men, cutlery, phones, computer mice, small books, jewellery, crayons, batteries, USB sticks, underwear, tinsel and elastic bands – in this room, the truth will always prevail.

Operating theatre

Bright lights, bizarre machines with tubes, lots of sharp things and people wearing masks – the stuff that doggy nightmares are made of.

Kennels

The vet calls them kennels. You'll call them cells. They serve two purposes: they're where you'll go when you're recovering from an operation and they provide an opportunity to experience life as a battery hen.

CANINE COMMENT

Belinda The thermometer goes WHERE?!

WALKIES

Humans have an idyllic view of what walkies should be like. This is based on a combination of watching too many Disney films and a misplaced sense of optimism and cheerfulness.

In your owner's mind, walkies involves a peaceful stroll through woodland with birds singing and squirrels and bunny rabbits going about their business, while man's loyal and obedient four-legged friend trots calmly and obediently at their side. The reality is somewhat different: the event tends to be less of a walk and more of a tug-of-war as they run the gauntlet of the local streets trying to stop you barking at other dogs, chasing cats and generally going where you shouldn't.

The truth about walkies is that they tend to involve an unstoppable force (you) meeting an immovable object (your owner). In this situation there can only ever be one winner and ensuring it's you comes down to how you position yourself. Walking at your owner's side or even behind him is unnatural and should be avoided at all costs. Positioning yourself in front means you can pull on your leash – a foolproof way to show who's boss and also control the speed and direction of travel.

In conclusion, when it comes to walkies, there's one essential piece of advice you must never, ever, ever forget: **Always walk your owner. Never let your owner walk you.**

How to recognize when it's time for walkies

The most obvious way you'll realize it's 'that time' is when your owner shouts, 'Walkies', while tantalizingly dangling your leash in front of you. However, there are also several non-verbal clues that every dog should look out for. These include your owner getting out of a chair, walking quite close to where your leash is hanging or going in the general direction of the front or back door.

Any of these actions can and should be taken as an indication that a walk is about to be offered. Bark loudly to indicate you understand your owner's intentions.

CANINE COMMENT

Jack Just remember this and you'll be okay: whoever's in front is in charge.

WARM SPOT

From what I gather, the Holy Grail for humans is a good parking spot. You'll probably hear your owners complaining about not being able to find one. The spot we're concerned with, though, is the warm spot which, comparatively speaking, is relatively straightforward to find.

Whether it's a bed, a couch or a chair, the warm spot is the area immediately under where your owner is sitting. As a human it's their job to create it; as a dog it's your duty to take it.

Essentially, your mission to take the warm spot relies on three things:

1. Patience
2. Cunning
3. Speed

153

Patience

You might be waiting for the warm spot for half an hour or more. Longer if your owner has good bladder control or is really engaged with the television show she's watching. You'll need to stay focused and not doze off: the window of opportunity to take the warm spot might only be a matter of seconds. If you're dreaming of chasing bunnies you'll miss it. You snooze, you lose.

Cunning

When it comes to a successful mission, cunning is everything. You'll need to decide where to position yourself and when and what to do if your intentions are discovered. You'll need to be able to think the whole process out from beginning to end and deal with unexpected changes to the plan (like your owner not deciding to make a cup of tea during a commercial break).

Speed

Where you position yourself will be a careful balance of a location that gives you a good vantage point, but is also within easy jumping distance of the warm spot when the time comes. As soon as your owner is out of the room, make your move with pace and purpose. He who hesitates is not only lost, but also destined to spend the rest of the evening on the cold floor.

WHEN YOU EVENTUALLY TAKE THE WARM SPOT

Stretch out, close your eyes and pretend to be asleep. If anyone pokes you or tries to move you, growl.

WASHING MACHINES

It might seem interesting and even intriguing the first time you see it in operation, but don't waste too much of your time staring at the washing machine. This is what you'll see:

- Human clothes going round one way
- Human clothes going round the other way

This is as good as it gets.

CANINE COMMENT

Louie Don't try this at home.

WASTE BINS

Forget rubber bones, squeaky slippers or balls with a bell inside them – waste bins are the best doggy toys, bar none. These are filled with discarded junk mail, envelopes, food wrappers, tissues, newspapers and apple cores, and it's fun to distribute the contents evenly throughout the whole house before your owners get home.

WORKING

Although most of us enjoy a leisurely life as a pampered pet, you might find yourself in the less fortunate position of having to work for a living. And as if that weren't bad enough, you'll find that just like greatness, some jobs are thrust upon you.

A few jobs are biased towards particular breeds, so if you're a Labrador with a good temperament you may well find yourself helping blind people; if you're an Alsatian then you're more suited to a job in the police; while if you're mangy and like barking and being tied to a post by an old rope, then a job guarding a scrap yard is probably your vocation.

Here are some of the opportunities available for dogs:

Drug sniffing

Pros: The glamour and prestige associated with taking down a Colombian drug cartel.

Cons: For every gram of cocaine you detect you'll have to sniff your way through several hundred kilos of dirty underwear.

Bomb sniffing

Pros: The excitement and thrill of a military career.

Cons: The spectacle and pageantry of a military funeral.

Guide dog

Pros: Your chance not only to help people, but also to get into cool places other dogs can't, like shops, pubs and restaurants.

Cons: A neon-coloured coat is always a fashion no-no.

Therapy dog

Pros: It's easy. All you have to do is go into care homes, hospitals and hospices and get petted and stroked.

Cons: While this is a very worthy and highly commendable career, it can be very depressing.

Showbiz

Pros: You can get to be a huge star like Lassie, Rin Tin Tin, Toto, Beethoven, Benjy, Digby, Hooch or Marley.

Cons: There's a danger that you'll end up less of a doggy actor and more of a performing monkey.

Corpse dog
Pros: The job title sounds really cool, almost like the title of a Tim Burton movie.
Cons: Traipsing through woodland or across an open heath can be energetic fun, but stumbling across a half-decomposed human body can take the edge off it.

Sheep dog
Pros: Lots of fresh air.
Cons: Lots of herding sheep.

Sled dog
Pros: A feeling of pioneering spirit as you race across an empty ice-covered wilderness.
Cons: It's so cold that if you lick your genitals your tongue will stick to them. Never a good look.

Gun dog
Pros: Plenty of time spent outdoors.
Cons: Not as glamorous as the job title sounds. You don't get to fire a gun; you do get to pick up dead birds in your mouth – and you can't keep them.

Fighting dog
Pros: Again, a cool-sounding job.
Cons: You'll be starved and there's a high likelihood of getting maimed or killed.

Police work

Pros: You get to jump up at criminals and bite them.
Cons: All that training palaver – running up ramps, through hoops and over walls. Too much like hard work.

Racing

Pros: Chasing a rabbit (or what passes for one) at high speed around an oval track while an enthusiastic crowd cheers you on … what's not to like?
Cons: Only open to greyhounds. Breed discrimination at its worst.

Guarding a scrap yard

Pros: You can bark and snarl as much as you want and no one will shout at you.
Cons: Discarded washing machines. Crushed cars. Broken televisions. The working environment is somewhat lacking in ambience.

CANINE COMMENT

Mishka The best thing about my job? Lots of opportunities to make yellow snow.

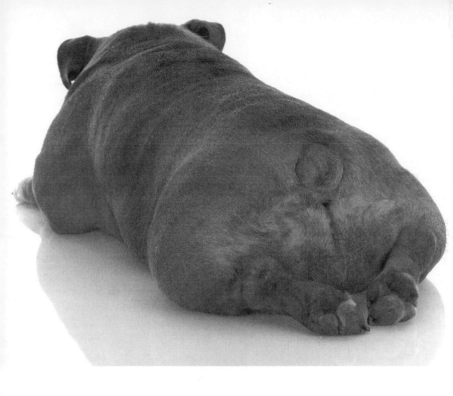

THE END